ISLAM
in the post 9/11 world

Copyright © 2003
First published 2004

All rights reserved. No part of this publication
may be reproduced in any form without prior
permission from the publisher.

British Library Cataloguing in Publication Data.
A catalogue record for this book is available
from the British Library.

ISBN 1-903921-21-X

Published by
Autumn House
Alma Park, Grantham, Lincs.
Printed in Thailand

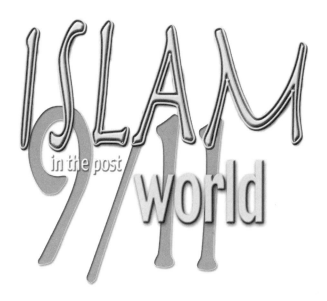

by Børge Schantz

Contents

Glossary

Introduction

Chapter 1
Time of ignorance. Life of Muhammad. Expansion of Islam 13
Time of ignorance 13
Muhammad, the prophet in Islam 14
The call to be a prophet 16
The flight to Medina 18
Mecca attacked and conquered. Ka'bah becomes the sanctuary of Islam 19
Life of Muhammad. His marriages 19
The history and expansion of Islam 21

Chapter 2
The Books of Islam 26
The Kor'an 26
The Kor'an described 28
Problems in the Kor'an 30
The Sunnah and the Hadith 31
Examples from the Hadith 33
Other Hadith excerpts 34

Chapter 3
Shari'ah Law 36
The Shar'iah, a comprehensive law system 37
The integrated society 38
The role of law 39
The foundations of Shar'iah law 40
Other influences on the Shar'iah 43

Chapter 4
Punishments for transgressions. Religious liberty. Fundamentalism 45
Specific punishments according to Shar'iah laws 45
Some observations 47
Old Testament penalties 47
Purpose is prevention 48

Mitigating circumstances 48
Primitive societies and severe punishments 49
The concept of religious liberty in Islam 50
Islamic fundamentalism 52

Chapter 5
The Five Pillars 54
1. The confession of faith (Shahada) 54
2. The ritual prayers (Salah) 55
3. Social taxation (Zak'ah) 58
4. The fast (Sawm) 59
5. The pilgrimage (Hajj) 61
Jihad, the holy war 64
Religion enhanced by body movements 65

Chapter 6
The Five Articles of Faith 67
1. The doctrine of Allah 67
2. The doctrine of angels 69
   The Jinn 70
3. Revealed scriptures 71
4. The messengers of Allah 72
5. Last events and the day of judgement 73
Predestination, the will of Allah 74

Chapter 7
The Muslim's Lifestyle 76
Childhood, youth, puberty and circumcision 76
Marriage 77
Death 78
The role of women in Islam 79
The dress of Muslim women 80
The Muslim marriage 82
Divorce, birth control and inheritance 83

Chapter 8
Diet, Art and Islamic Sects 86
The Kor'anic dietary plan for animal consumption 86
Cultic health principles 88
Other areas of the Muslim lifestyle 89

Reasons for variations in Muslim patterns of life 92
Islamic sects 92
Folk Islam 93
Sufism – the mysticism in Islam 95

Chapter 9
Islam in the 21st Century 96
The Mediterranean Sea 96
The Ottoman Empire – Colonial Era 97
The years after the Second World War 99
The two chief reasons for dissatisfaction 101
The Call to Jihad 103
The "Abode of War", the "Abode of Islam" 105
Suicide terrorists or martyrs? 108

Chapter 10
Muslims in the West 110
First contact 110
Second contact 111
Third contact 111
Fourth contact 112
Economic refugees 113
Why the West? 114
Muslims among Christians 115
Assimilation, integration, clashes of cultures 115
Elements of culture clash 116
Culture clash and Shar'iah law 117
Child abduction 118
Law as a personal responsibility 118
When in Rome, do as the Romans do 119
Juvenile delinquency 119

Chapter 11
Reformation, coexistence 121
Corruption, poverty and humiliation 121
Science and economy 122
Dissatisfaction on the edges of the Islamic world 123
Liberals and Fundamentalists 124
Is coexistence at all possible? 125
What about the future? 127

The Shar'iah law can be observed only in a Muslim country 127
There are Muslims and Muslims 129
The conflict between the Shar'iah and Western lifestyle 131
Hope – perhaps 132

Chapter 12
A Christian meets a Muslim 135
The Great Commission 136
Mission in Muslim lands 136
Unsuccessful mission among Muslims in Christian nations 137
Muslims among us are in a state of transition 139
Variable attitudes 139
Friendship 141
Knowledge and information 142
Hospitality 142
Listen and learn 143
Personal conversations 144
The extended family 144
Loss of face can mean loss of faith 145
Avoid criticism 145
Dreams as part of a Muslim's religious experience 146

Chapter 13
Christian and Muslim beliefs 147
The Sovereign Allah 147
The ninety-nine names of Allah 148
Predestination 149
Jesus Christ 150
The concept of sin 152
The conception of salvation 155

Conclusion 158

Bibliography 163

Glossary

adda .... perform a religious ritual
adhan .... call to public prayer
'adl .... just, of good character
'ahd .... covenant; agreement
ahl al-kitab .... people of the book, Jews and Christians
ahmadiyah .... Islamic sect. Ikke anerkendt
'alamat .... sign, often in a dream
Allah .... God
'arraf .... diviner, fortune-teller
ayat .... verse in the Kor'an: sign from heaven
'ayatollah .... Shi'ite doctor of Islamic law
baraka .... blessing
bismillah .... in the name of God
dar al-Harb .... the abode, land of war. Areas where Islam is not ruling
dar al-Islam .... the abode, land of Islam. Areas where Islam is ruling
dawah .... Islamic missionary activity
derwish .... a Sufi miracle worker
dhimmi .... a person of another religion approved by Islam
din .... religion
du'a .... a personal prayer
Fatiha .... the opening sura of the Kor'an
ghusl .... ablution of the whole body
hadith .... traditions; what Muhammad said, did, approved of; something said in his presence
hajj .... pilgrimage to Mecca
Hajji .... a person who has completed the hajj
halal .... lawful; legal
hanif .... pre-Islamic Arab monotheist
haram .... forbidden; unlawful
hijab .... covering dress of Muslim women
hijrah .... Muhammad's flight from Mecca to Medina AD622.

ibadat	worship
Iblis	the devil
ihram	the dress worn for pilgrimage to Mecca. State of purity
ijma	the consensus of the religious community
imam	leader of the mosque; leader of the Shi'ite community
insha'llah	if Allah wills. Expression of man's dependence on Allah
Injil	The Gospels or New Testament
Isa	Jesus
Islam	to submit; submission
isnad	the chain of authority of the Hadith
jahiliya	the pre-Islamic age of ignorance before Muhammad
Jibra'il	the angel Gabriel
jihad	to strive for spiritual purity; a holy war against self or unbelievers in the name of Allah with word or sword
jinn	spirits created by Allah, some good and others evil
Ka'bah	the black stone at Mecca
kafir	unbeliever, infidel
khatib	religious leader who preaches in the mosque
kufr	to deny God
mahdi	a saviour who comes to rescue and guide
majdhub	a holy man who has spontaneous illumination
Mikha'il	the angel Michael
mubah	open to individual choice in following the law
muezzin	the one who calls to prayer
mufti	an Islamic leader and a legal consultant of Islamic law
mullah	a religious leader in Iran, India and Pakistan
muta	temporary marriage
nabi	prophet sent by Allah with a message
nubuwwah	prophecy
qadi	judge; religious judge

qiblah	direction of the Ka'bah in Mecca
rakahs	bowing up and down in praying; prostration
Ramadan	the fast month; ninth month of the Muslim calendar
rasul	apostle; messenger
riba	usury
sadaqah	charity; alms
salat	prayers or worship prescribed five times daily for Muslims
sawm	fasting
shahada	the confession: there is no god but Allah and Muhammed is Allah's messenger
shar'iah	Islamic law based upon the Kor'an and Hadith
shaytan	the devil; Satan
shirk	associating others with Allah, eg associating Jesus with God
Sufism	the mystical movement in Islam
sunnah	habits, customs and sayings of Muhammed and his disciples
surah	a chapter in the Kor'an
tanzil	the way the Kor'an was presented to Muhammed
taqiyyah	hiding of one's religious beliefs in the face of danger
tawhid	monotheism, doctrine of one God
Tawrat	Torah, Books of Moses
ul'ama	scholars of law
ummah	the community of believers
wudu	ritual washing; cleansing before prayer
Zabur	Psalms
zakat	alms; tithe to help the poor, fighters for Islam, and care for travelling guests

Introduction

Islam in the Post-9/11 World is not a completely neutral book, even though I have been as objective as possible in my description of Islam and my comparisons with Christianity. The undeniable fact that I am a Christian missionary, who has worked for many years in Islamic areas, and studied Islam as a specialist subject, has inevitably influenced my approach to this book. *Islam in the Post-9/11 World* is a book written by a Christian for Christians.

In the early chapters, the history of Islam and the beliefs and lifestyles of Muslims are dealt with. Special emphasis is placed on the *Shar'iah*, the Islamic law, that plays an important role and is a leading principle in the religion of Muslims. It is the Muslim's all-embracing guide, dealing with his lifestyle, family affairs, economic and judicial questions, his relationship with other Muslims and adherents of other religions.

An account of the beliefs and lifestyles can be fully understood only when an elementary knowledge of the *Shar'iah* is appreciated. This law, interpreted in its extreme form, is the reason why a smooth integration of Muslims into Christian societies is a difficult, even impossible, task. For these reasons endeavours have been made to provide a detailed description of the *Shar'iah*. The author is convinced that the *Shar'iah* in the wrong hands – and interpreted in excessive detail – has led to violent confrontations.

The questions in regard to assimilation, integration, culture clashes, even co-existence, are treated with one main purpose: to ascertain how biblical ideals and Christian attitudes can help in the new and delicate situation. The book also deals with the problems a Muslim is facing when living in a society where *Shar'iah* is not the legal tender. The last chapters will give some suggestions as to how to go about witnessing for one's faith to Muslim friends and neighbours.

Like Christianity, Islam is divided into many sects with various ways of practising the religion. With this in mind I have tried to be general in my treatment of the subjects and find a common denominator that in a reasonable way covers what Muslims in general stand for. This has not been an easy task.

In the text I have deliberately, for the sake of the readers, used the Arabic word for God, Allah, in connection with the concepts of the deity in Islam. The word God is applied when I deal with Christian concepts. The Arabic words used in the text will be followed by the English equivalent. In the Glossary some commonly used Arabic words are explained in more detail. In the text itself there will be very few references to literature on the subject. My studies of Islam stretch over a long period and I have, over many years, consulted books and articles in various languages. It has not been possible for me to quote accurately the many thoughts, interpretations and ideas in the various works. It is also difficult at times to recall whether an observation is one I have made myself, heard in a lecture or read in a book or article. At the end of the book there will be a general bibliography.

I am grateful to the many unknown authors, Christian, secular and Muslim, who all in their own way have helped me to get a better understanding of Islam. They have often challenged my Christian beliefs. However, generally the result has been that my Christian commitment is strengthened.

The author has reason to thank the many who have patiently helped him in his attempts to use the English language as a vehicle of expression. These helpful persons have also pointed out weaknesses in the arguments and points that needed further explanation.

Børge Schantz
Vemmedrup, Denmark, September 2003

chapter 1

Time of ignorance before Muhammad
The life of Muhammad
Expansion of Islam

Islam has its roots in the Arabian Peninsula, much of which today is Saudi Arabia. One thousand five hundred years ago this was a sparsely-populated region with a scattered Bedouin population, often engaged in hostilities with one another as they fought for the resources of water and feed for camels, horses, donkeys, goats and sheep. This peninsula – twelve times the size of the United Kingdom and less than one third the size of the USA – had one main city, Mecca. Not only did the Bedouins do their business there; it was a place from which caravans started out or made their stopover, and it was also a religious centre.

Time of ignorance

In Mecca was the *Ka'bah*, a sanctuary where all the idols from the many Bedouin clans, about 360, were to be found. Mecca was also a place with the most degrading practices and immoral behaviour in business and private life. Slavery was common. Blood feuds and murder were daily occurrences. The poor suffered from all kinds of humiliation and exploitation. Muhammad called the time before the advent of Islam *Jahiliyyah* (the time of ignorance).

Around the desert peninsula were well-organised

nations and empires. To the north was the Byzantine Empire, with its orthodox Christian tradition. To the west was the Ethiopian kingdom, with its Coptic Christian tradition. Persia, on the other side of the Gulf to the east of the Arabian peninsula, had Zoroastrianism, based on the worship of a High God, and the belief that good thoughts, words and deeds were the highest virtues.

The Arabs also worshipped a High God, who was the creator. At the same time they worshipped lesser deities, even female gods. Images and statues in the *Ka'bah* in Mecca represented the most important deities. In addition they believed in the *jinn* (supernatural beings, both friendly and hostile. Children will be familiar with the story of the jinn's appearing from Aladdin's lamp). There were small sanctuaries in various places in the desert, where these deities and spirits were worshipped after certain rituals. The main worship rituals and services took place in Mecca at the *Ka'bah*. The Arabic language was, in an interesting fashion, tied to religion through poetry and proverbs.

Also in the Arabian desert lived Jewish tribes that had been there since 722BC. In addition, from a subsequent period, there were various Christian sects of the Roman Catholic and Greek Orthodox traditions with their priests, monks, churches, schools and monasteries. Even though the many smaller Bedouin clans were constantly fighting one another, they agreed to lay aside all discords when they met in Mecca to worship their various High Gods. At the same time, the pilgrimage to the *Ka'bah* provided an opportunity to do business with the merchants in Mecca.

Muhammad, the prophet in Islam

In Mecca, this town in the middle of the desert, far away from the cultural centres with organised religion,

Muhammad was born. He entered a cultural and spiritual vacuum that was to change not only his life but the lives of thousands ever since. Muslims have tried to reconstruct the life of Muhammad, the prophet of Islam. The life of this ancient founder of a monotheistic religion is the one we know most about. We have many more details of Muhammad's life in the Islamic tradition *Sunnah*, than we have of the life of Jesus Christ in the Christian record.

Nevertheless, Muhammad's life story, as we have it, is a strange mixture of facts, folklore and myths about supernatural happenings. One has to read a lot of hagiography in order to distinguish between fact and imagination. The use of common sense is essential in separating folklore from fact.

The most important events in the life of Muhammad and the beginning of the history of Islam, according to the most reliable Islamic sources, can be listed as follows. They are dated in accordance with the Christian chronology.

Birth 570
Orphan 576
Marriage to Khadijah 595
Call to be a prophet. First vision 610
Khadijah's death 620
Flight to Medina, inauguration of first Islamic State, and year 1 in Islamic calendar 622
Jihad (holy war instituted) 623
Five wars against Mecca 623-628
Conquest of Mecca 629
Death of Muhammad 632

Muhammad was born into a poor family in Mecca, of the Hashemite clan and the Quaraysh family. His father

Abdullah died before his birth; his mother Amina died before he reached 6 years of age. His grandfather took over the responsibility of bringing up the boy, but he died before Muhammad reached maturity. As early as 12 years of age, the orphaned boy joined the extensive caravan traffic that had Mecca as its focus. Mecca was the natural oasis for caravans between Yemen and Damascus. On at least two occasions, Muhammad visited Syria as a camel-driver. On these trips through the desert it is claimed that Muhammad met with Christian monks and heard them preach and teach. These monks, no doubt, belonged to various sects within the main traditions. They lived far away from Rome or Constantinople, and it's possible that their preaching and doctrines at times diverged from the main teaching of their respective churches, which could explain why the paraphrases of the biblical accounts in the Kor'an are often distorted past recognition.

Muhammad was a diligent, honest and intelligent young man, and Khadijah, the female owner of the caravan enterprise, noticed him. When he was 25 years old she made him an offer of marriage, and thus Muhammad's first wife was a financially independent business woman fifteen years his senior.

The call to be a prophet

Muhammad, a spiritual person with a strong sense of justice, felt called to fight against the immorality, polytheism, idolatry and shady business methods so rampant in Mecca. He spent much time in solitude and meditation. According to Islamic tradition, it was during one of these meditations – in a cave outside Mecca – that he had his first vision. The archangel Gabriel was sent to him by Allah. On this occasion he was shown the whole Kor'an, and was called to be a prophet of Allah. Muhammad, however, wondered whether the call was from Allah or Iblis (Satan). Khadijah had a relative who had accepted Christianity in the Time of Ignorance. He was consulted, and expressed the thought that Allah was calling him. It was in this way that a Christian confirmed Muhammad's call to be the prophet of Islam.

During the next twenty-two years the Kor'an was revealed to Muhammad piecemeal in a series of visions. Tradition has it that Muhammad was illiterate, as many Arabs were at his time. Perhaps the prophet's illiteracy is an advantage for Islam. The less schooling the prophet has enjoyed, the more the prophecy can be attributed to divine origin. After the visions Muhammad was able to dictate word for word what he had heard from Gabriel. Companions wrote down his words, using parchment, potsherds, palm leaves, bones and animal skins.

These fragments recording the visions were secretly scattered and hidden all over Mecca. The merchants did not welcome the teaching of Muhammad, in which a belief in Allah as the only god supplanted the worship of about 360 gods and idols housed in the *Ka'bah*! It meant that the temple in Mecca would no longer be the place of worship for the many Bedouin tribes. That, in turn, led to their losing some of their business, as Bedouins used pilgrimages to sell skins and meat, and buy salt, sugar and whatever was available to help them make the hard desert life more pleasant. Muhammad and the first preachers of monotheism and a better moral code were met with much resistance.

The pioneers in Islam had to work underground; some fled for their lives to Ethiopia, where a Coptic Christian emperor gave them protection and shelter.

The flight to Medina

Twelve years after his first vision in 622, the prophet had to flee to a more secure place. He travelled secretly to Medina, a town about 200 miles north of Mecca, and Medina became the centre for Muhammad's activities until his death in 632. This flight is called the *Hijrah* (Arabic for migration), and marks year one in the Muslim calendar.

In the town there were already a few followers of the new religion and the prophet was welcomed. Arabs and Jews saw in Muhammad a much-needed leader for their community. There were the usual disputes in the city between the various religious groups and tribal factions, and the citizens felt that a stranger such as Muhammad could help redress their grievances.

With Muhammad as the patriarch and prophet, Medina society slowly developed into a theocracy. In one and the same person the roles and offices of prophet, lawgiver, judge, mayor, commander of the army and teacher came to be embodied.

Islam has three holy cities: Mecca, Medina and Jerusalem. Mecca is the spiritual centre where pilgrims meet to worship. It was also the place where Muslims met heavy resistance and persecution when they preached their new doctrine that there was only one god, Allah. Medina, by contrast, was the town where Islam unfolded and expanded. It was there that the ideal Islamic state was first established and where strict rules could be adhered to without hindrance or interference. For that reason, Medina became for Muslims in all places and in all ages the symbol of the rule of Allah on earth.

Jerusalem was esteemed because of its connection with the prophets of the Old Testament, approved by Islam – a status enhanced because Muhammad is said to have visited the city at night, when the archangel miraculously brought him there. Muslim tradition has it that the prophet left his footprint on the Temple Mount when he ascended.

Mecca attacked and conquered
Ka'bah becomes the sanctuary of Islam

From Medina the Muslims, under the leadership of Muhammad, attacked the Meccan caravans in several battles with the rich merchants. In 630 the people from Medina captured Mecca with little bloodshed. Muhammad's first act when he entered the town was to visit the *Ka'bah* and to rid the sanctuary of all the idols, which were thrown out and crushed or burned. The *Ka'bah* was then declared the centre of worship for all Muslims and Allah was declared the only God.

The *Ka'bah* was a building that, according to Muslim tradition, was built by Adam and his son Seth. As time passed, and people backslid from the true religion, the building became dilapidated. It was rebuilt by Abraham and Ishmael. Muhammad was the last prophet to cleanse the building from all iniquity and reinstate the *Ka'bah* as the sanctuary of Islam.

The building was cubical with a length, breadth and height of about forty feet. In one corner stood a large black stone, ten inches in diameter, which was given by Gabriel to Abraham. Pilgrims to Mecca were expected to kiss the black stone, or at least show respect for it when passing. Only Muslims had access to Mecca. Millions of pilgrims from the Islamic world still visit their holy city each year.

The life of Muhammad
His marriages

Having conquered Mecca, Muhammad returned to Medina

where he stayed. He continued with his work as both spiritual and temporal leader of the town and as prophet and reformer in the Arab community until his death two years later in 632.

His marriage to Khadijah lasted twenty-five years until she passed away in 620, at 65 years of age. As long as she was alive Muhammad married no other women, although polygamy was common in Arabic societies before Islam was introduced.

Muhammad married thirteen women in total – eleven wives and two concubines. Islam allows a man to have up to four wives. An exception was made in the case of the prophet of Islam who had nine wives at the same time. The youngest and last wife Muhammad married was Aisha. She was only 6 years old when he married her and 9 when the marriage was consummated. His marriages can, to some extent, be regarded as social arrangements and unions. Companions were killed in war, and widows and daughters left without support. By allowing Muslim companions to marry them, Islam ensured that they were accorded status in society and security. Some of the prophet's marriages also served political ends. Muhammad united his companions and Bedouin clans to himself by marrying their daughters. Perhaps some of his marriages served to strengthen *international* ties. One of his wives was a gift from the Ethiopian emperor. Her name was Miriam (Mary) and she was Coptic, the only Christian in his harem. His tenth wife was a 17-year-old Jewish girl who converted to Islam.

It is worth noticing that from his thirteen marriages only six children were born. And they all had one mother – Khadijah. It is interesting to observe that a woman who had passed 40 years of age gave birth to six children, in a time and place where hygiene and medical science were not too far advanced.

Muhammad's other twelve wives, therefore, yielded no heirs. Khadijah gave him two sons and four daughters, all born before Muhammad was called to be a prophet. The boys died in infancy, and only one of the daughters, Fatima, had children of her own. Muslim theologians explain this interesting situation as an intervention from Allah for the sake of the peaceful co-existence of future Muslims, as no Muslims can claim that they are direct descendants of Muhammad in the male line. The kings of Morocco and Jordan claim to be the descendants of the prophet of Islam through the line of his daughter Fatima. However, that does not really count for much in the Islamic law of heredity, where things pass down only through the male line.

The history and expansion of Islam

The religion Muhammad founded in the seventh century is called Islam (submission to Allah). In his lifetime the prophet succeeded, with the help of the new religion, in gathering the many Bedouin tribes and clans into one people, speaking the same language, Arabic. Islam as a religion took over the role that tribal allegiance had formerly played.

The religion with Muhammad as the last prophet, with the Kor'an as the seal of the revelations of Allah, is essentially universal. Islam is meant to be proclaimed to all peoples. Early in the history of Islam the Arabic Muslims began, in different ways, not only to share their newfound religion with fellow tribespeople; but to extend their faith to neighbouring nations. The 'broadcasting' of the faith was generally by peaceful means with words of persuasion, but there were cases where force was used to gain proselytes. Christians, however, should not be too self-righteous in this respect. They, too, have sometimes used arms – and even bribery – as a means of 'conversion'.

Only a hundred years after the death of Muhammad, Islam had adherents not only in Arabia but also in parts of Asia, India and North Africa. Islam had also crossed the Mediterranean and gained a foothold in Europe. Sicily and great parts of what today we call Spain, Portugal and France were under Muslim sovereignty. During the following centuries Islam spread as far as the Pacific Ocean. The conquest continued to the extent that, by the advent of the twentieth century Islam had become the main religion in a belt north of the Equator stretching from Morocco to Indonesia. In broad outline the expansion can roughly be outlined as follows:

The four righteous caliphs of Medina. 632-661. Islam reaches Palestine, Syria, Egypt, North Africa, Iraq and Iran.

The Umayyad caliphs of Damascus. 661-750. Further expansions into Spain, Southern France, Turkey and Central Asia.

The Abbassid caliphs of Baghdad claimed descent from Abbas, Muhammad's uncle. 750-1258. The golden, glorious age of Islam, but was followed by 500 years of disunity that led to a decline in political influence, science and thought.

The Mamelukes of Cairo. 1258-1517. Time of the Crusades (1096-1258). Mongols conquer Iraq and Iran.

The Ottomans of Istanbul. 1517-1919. Expansions into India, Malaysia and Indonesia. At the end of this period most Muslim areas came under colonial (Christian) sovereignty.

The modern world. 1919 - . Islamic nations gain their independence after World War II. Numerous internal squabbles in the Middle East. Oil attains international political importance. Tensions with non-Muslims result in terror attacks.

The Muslims reached a cultural and scientific zenith during the time of the Abbassid caliphs (750-1258). The ninth and tenth centuries marked a glorious age for Islam when the Arab elite kept the torch of knowledge burning in Muslim areas. While we in Europe were experiencing what has been termed 'the Dark Ages', universities and libraries were founded in Islamic cities. Art, architecture, astronomy, medical science and other branches of scholarship flowered among Islamic peoples. Ironically, the science that blossomed among the Muslims was to some extent based on European, especially Greek, sources. Arab scholars had translated scientific works from Greek to Arabic. In the Renaissance these works were 'returned' to Europe, where they were further developed.

Political decline caused cultural and scientific stagnation among the Muslims. They also lost their previous military strength.

Islamic peoples were humiliated in the nineteenth century when Muslim countries came under European colonial sovereignty. By 1900 Christian nations such as Great Britain, France, the Netherlands, Italy, Russia and Spain ruled the Islamic world. Often they ruled with a heavy hand and exploited the resources to their own selfish ends. After the Second World War most of the Islamic nations received their independence and had the task of finding their place in history and their way into the modern world. This development did not take place without birth pangs, problems, confrontations and both external and internal conflicts, often resulting in terror attacks and other variations on violence. Many Muslims in all Islamic nations are depressed over the failure of their attempts to obtain a decent standard of living. One of the main issues is their experience of one defeat after another in the wars with Israel. Other dilemmas are the undemocratic, often corrupt, Islamic governments that use religion and the words of the Kor'an to keep Muslim people in submission. Some Muslims are convinced that the way forward is to return to the classical Islam practised 1,400 years ago.

For eighty years Arab nationalism was the great hope. The idea was to abolish all borders between Muslim countries and establish one brotherhood living in accordance with *Shar'iah* laws. That proved an illusion. For fifty years after that it appeared that friendship with the atheistic Soviet Union was the great hope. However, the arms supplied by the Communists were insufficient and outmoded, then the Communist system itself collapsed.

A quarter of a century ago Muslims thought that the oil would produce the power and wealth they wanted so badly, but even there they had no success.

It is understandable that today's modern ambitious Muslims have the feeling that the world has been unfair to them and their people. As a consequence, they have come to the conclusion that 'true Islam' is the only comfort, the only way forward and the only hope – using their religion to hit back at the myriad injustices Muslims feel they have suffered, which helps to explain the 11 September attacks.

For centuries Muslims and Christians lived apart from one another. The isolation was not caused merely by oceans and deserts. There were also the dangers and difficulties of transportation and communication. Today the situation is quite different. Although 1.2 billion Muslims live in a little more than fifty Islamic nations in an area between the 10th and 40th latitude, from the Atlantic Ocean to the Pacific Ocean, many Muslims have taken up residence in Europe and North America. In various places and for various reasons they have arrived during the last four decades in Christian countries with a high standard of living. We meet them on the streets, at work, in the classroom and in the market places.

Their reasons for being in Europe and North America vary considerably. The majority were invited to help on the expanding labour market at a time when there were few local workers to fill the positions. Some were refugees from political or religious persecution. Students came to take advantage of higher education not available in their home countries. Others were legitimate immigrants suffering from persecution and seeking a new life in the Western world. Finally there are the so-called 'refugees of convenience' who crossed the borders in order to exploit the social benefits of our societies.

It is loosely estimated that there are 1.2 billion Muslims in the world today. That means that 20% of the world's population pray in the direction of Mecca. Of these about 300 million live in non-Islamic areas. Quite a few Muslims are in Christian nations.

chapter 2
The books of Islam

Islam and Christianity both claim to be divinely inspired. Both claim that divinity has taken the initiative or at least co-operated with man in making a divine plan. To Muslims the rules for life and the road to eternal salvation were revealed by Allah to Muhammad through the archangel Gabriel. The revelation was written down in the Kor'an. Over twenty-two years the content of the Kor'an was communicated to the prophet piecemeal. Muhammad dictated the fragments to his companions. Hostilities on the part of the Meccans caused these fragments to be scattered and hidden in many places all over the town.

The Kor'an

The son-in-law of Muhammad, khalif Uthman, took upon himself the tedious task of collecting all the fragments and editing them. In that way, twenty years after the death of Muhammad, the Kor'an took shape. Whatever did not become part of the 'canon' was destroyed. Although the Kor'an translators claim that this was the case, some Muslims deny that it happened. By this act of destruction the scholars in Islam, once and for all, closed discussion concerning what should and should not have been accepted in the Kor'an. It would have been interesting and enlightening if they had kept the 'left-overs'. These pieces of information would have provided an insight into what people at the time of Muhammad were thinking, together with their views of the prophet and the new religion.

The Kor'an is accepted as the complete and final revelation from Allah to all mankind. It is claimed to be an exact reproduction of the original engraved tablets in heaven, written in the language some Muslims regard as the language of the angels, Arabic. The text is believed to be perfect and holy. For that very reason only an archangel, Gabriel, could be trusted to communicate the message from Allah to the new prophet, Muhammad. Neither he nor any other human being had any share in the content of the Kor'an or its origination.

That is one reason why the Kor'an is regarded as authoritative only when it is read in Arabic. In this way the Arabic language attained its outstanding position among the languages of the world. The belief that every word came directly from the throne of Allah has resulted in some Muslim scholars' claim that the Kor'an was not 'created', but had co-existed with the divinity from eternity. This Islamic concept of divinity reminds us of the Christian *trinity* concept, which Muslims, however, regard as polytheism (belief in more than one god).

It is held that every word in the Kor'an was especially selected to express the divine will and Allah's plan for mankind. It is believed to be the only true source for doctrine and science and the only valid guide for life because every word came from the very throne of Allah. Muslims believe in a kind of 'verbal-inspiration'. They hold that the words of the Kor'an in themselves have the authority for understanding and interpretation. Most Christians accept that no human language is perfect and hence believe in some kind of 'idea-inspiration' — that the meaning behind the words is inspired, not necessarily the individual words. For that reason a Christian will, in a discussion with a Muslim, often fall into the trap of the 'battle of the books', the Bible versus the Kor'an.

In the Bible versus the Kor'an discussion it must always be remembered that the Muslim believes that the Kor'an is a perfect book, sent from heaven as the unadulterated words of Allah. Most Christians, however, believe that the Bible as God's word is only one of the ways in which God chooses to communicate with man. For Muslims, the Kor'an is the *most important* means of transmitting messages from heaven, but most Christians do not claim that the Bible as literature is perfect, even when they honour it as the inspired word of God. Christians claim that the Holy Spirit used erring humans as spokespersons. As 'mortal tools' they kept their own way of writing. None of them claimed perfection. Christians believe that the greatest revelation of God to mankind is not in a book, but *in the person of Jesus Christ* revealed *in* the book. The difference in concepts can be summarised thus: in Islam the word of Allah became a *book*; in Christianity it became *flesh*, when Christ was born (John 1:14). The Kor'an, the book from heaven, is for the Muslim the most perfect object in the world. The Christian honours Christ as the only perfect man this sinful world has known.

The Kor'an described

The Arabic from which we have the word Kor'an means 'to recite'. Muslims believe that Allah communicated with all people, especially the Jews, before Muhammad was born. Allah called the Jews and Christians, it is claimed. They had their holy books, the Torah and the Gospel. However, the

Muslims believe that Jews and Christians tampered with both the Old and the New Testaments, which was why Muhammad was called to be a prophet, to revive the true message from Allah and replace the 'corrupted' Bible with the true and unadulterated Word.

A 'Higher Kor'an Criticism' is not allowed, and a Muslim has no right to listen to one. Christian scholars are, of course, not bound by such prohibitions. They have come to the conclusion that the Old and the New Testaments, as well as Jewish writings and other sources, have influenced the Kor'an. They have also discovered idioms and words in the Kor'an text that were borrowed from non-Arabic languages such as Greek, Persian, Turkish, and even Hindi. When one reads the Kor'an, one soon discovers that life in the desert and the oasis, as well as Meccan trade and judicial language and images, has had its influence.

The Kor'an is the same size as the New Testament, about 300 pages. It is divided into 114 *Surahs*. *Surah* means section. They have names such as The Cow, Mary, Women, and Jonah. In the same way, Christians and Jews have divided up the Bible. The *Surahs* are not set down in chronological order. The longest are first in the Kor'an, the shortest at the end. The *Surahs* are again divided into verses (*ayats*) of which there are more than 6,000. The Kor'an was written over a period of twenty-two years. It must be considered as unfit for historical studies, even though some parts are based on events in the life of Muhammad in the Arabian Peninsula. The Kor'an is a collection of exhortations, warnings, and rules for family life, worship and prayer. It is Allah's call, through the prophet Muhammad, to all people to return to the true faith. At the same time it is believed to contain the rules by which our personal lives should be ordered. Some Muslims also claim that in the Kor'an there are the principles of true science, education and law.

During the twelve years Muhammad and his companions spent in Mecca they were persecuted and ridiculed. This gave rise to the longer *Surahs* with their theology and prayers to Allah for protection and revenge over the enemies of the new religion. The last ten years of Muhammad's life were spent in Medina. There he was not only a prophet, but the mayor and military commander. And there he wrote about the practical aspects of the Muslim life.

In the shorter *Surahs* we find counsel on how to be a Muslim. In the Medina-*Surahs* there are rules for property rights and inheritance. Marriage and family matters take up to 30% of the *ayats*. It is worth noting that only about 500 verses out of more than 6,000 speak directly about law.

Problems in the Kor'an

The Kor'an is esteemed as a perfect book, with revelations directly from Allah. Every word is considered inspired – passed on in a miraculous manner. To the Muslim, the Kor'an has in it supernatural power. The book is kept over the door-frame wrapped in silk and touched only after a ceremonial cleansing. As a preparation for special occasions the Muslim will keep the Kor'an near to his heart. Students will place their copies under their pillows on the night prior to sitting for examinations.

The Kor'an is translated into many languages, though for centuries this was forbidden. The teaching was that the Kor'an should appear only in Arabic. Christians who wished to study Islam made the first translations. Today, by a royal decree, the Custodian of the Two Holy Mosques, the King of Saudi Arabia, has authorised translation of the

Kor'an into several languages, on the understanding that they are termed 'translations of *the meaning* of the Kor'an', not translations of the Kor'an itself. Only the Arabic text has authority and should be used in worship. Today there are about 200 translations, though not all are approved by the King of Saudi Arabia.

As mentioned, Muslims claim that the Kor'an is perfect, originating with Allah and called the Mother of Books. For that reason it is considered blasphemous to be involved in any criticism of the book, let alone in any attempt to prove its infallibility by the use of archaeological digs or studies into history.

There are, however, mistakes and contradictions in the Kor'an. One dilemma is the punishment for adultery, especially for women. In *Surah* 24:2 it is 100 lashes with the whip, while *Surah* 4:15 puts the penalty at house arrest for life. Did Allah, who is eternal and perfect, really change his mind within a span of 22 years, the time it took to communicate the Kor'an to Muhammad?

Muslims can and will point out certain contradictions and inaccuracies in the Bible. And rightly so. Most Christians, however, will never maintain that the Bible is a perfect book. 'The Holy Scriptures, which are able to make you wise for salvation' (2 Tim. 3:15), were revealed to imperfect men, who wrote in imperfect earthly languages.

The *Sunnah* and the *Hadith*

The Kor'an, with only about 300 pages, does not have the answers and solutions to all questions and problems in the life of a Muslim. It does not cover all aspects of religious, social, economic or family life. In Islamic teaching it is believed that a prophet, from the moment he is called, lives a righteous life and is a perfect example to be followed.

This belief made an important contribution to Islamic teachings and rendered much easier to understand the rules for Muslim life and behaviour.

More is known about the life of Muhammad than about the founder of any other world religion. What Muhammad or, for that matter, his first companions said or did, whom they met, what they approved or condemned, even ignored, could all be imitated safely. The word *Sunnah* means custom, habit or usage. The *Sunnah*, based on the life, teachings and activities of Muhammad, was elevated as the ideal in the life of a Muslim. In many cases it became an unwritten law.

As time passed these *Sunnahs* increased prodigiously. It is estimated that 250 years after the death of Muhammad 750,000 circulated. In those days some Muslims used the false *Sunnahs* to defend all kinds of heresies and religious attitudes, contrary to what was regarded as orthodox Islam. For this reason it was necessary to collect the true *Sunnahs* and get them authorised. These collections were called *Hadith*, which means reports or accounts. The task of collecting these sayings and organising them into books 150-250 years after the event was a very complicated and demanding task. It meant that the *Hadith* collectors, and there were many of them, had to reconstruct a chain (*isnad*) of men – backward from the penman to the eye-witness – who had had a consecutive connection with one another since Muhammad. In most cases this involved five or six generations.

There were several classes of trustworthiness in the *Hadith*, all depending on the reliability of the men in the chain. In order to be accepted as a *Hadith*, the saying had to agree with the Kor'an, agree with first-class *Sunnahs*, and be reasonable.

This research resulted in six major – and numerous minor – *Hadith* collections. There was a difference between those *Hadiths* accepted by the *Shi'ites* and the *Sunnis*. Best known is the nine volume *al-Bukhari* collection with more than 9,000 articles. This collection was ready 200 years after the death of Muhammad.

The *Hadiths* deal with additional revelations from Allah through the prophet, commentaries on the Kor'an, explanations of doctrines, religious and social conditions, attacks on non-Muslims, and teachings about the last events in history and the day of judgement. The *Hadith* also presents detailed counsel concerning the Muslim's daily life, funeral rituals, dietary regulations and hospitality. There are even *Hadiths* on such trivial matters as how one binds sandals, sneezes and dresses. The *Hadith* gives a great deal of information about Muhammad's private life and marriages.

Examples from the *Hadith*

In the *al-Timidhi* collection (around AD850, or 250 years after the death of Muhammad) we find an interesting example that shows not only how the chain works. It also reveals Muhammad's outstanding comprehension of the conditions needed for starting a new religious movement, but also the way the cause grows:

> *In the beginning, if one omits a tenth of the law, one will be punished,*
> *but at the end of time if one accomplishes a tenth of the law, one will be saved.*

The chain is as follows:
Among the companions who heard the prophet utter these words were:
Abu Huraryah
> who told it to

Al-A'Raj
> who told it to
Abu Zinaad
> who told it to
Sufian Ibn U'aynah
> who told it to
Muain Ibn Hammad
> who told it to
Ibrahim Abu Yakoub Al-Jouzjani
> who wrote it down.

The chain reveals six generations of Muslims. At the time it must have entailed considerable research to determine each person's reliability. After all, these people lived up to 250 years prior to the writing of the *Hadith*.

The *Hadiths* are officially inferior to the Kor'an, but in reality many Muslims put them on the same level as their holy book.

Other *Hadith* excerpts

On the bringing up of children:
> *The mind of a newborn is like a vacant land, which accepts every seed that is sown in it.*
>
> *For seven years a child should play; for another seven years he should be taught how to read and write and for still another seven years he shall learn about lawful and unlawful things.*

A *Hadith* on cleanliness and health:
> *Do not drink water from a broken vessel and similarly from its handle because Satan sits there.*
>
> *Keeping one's house clean removes poverty and helplessness.*

On women:
> *When a man marries a woman for her wealth and*

> beauty Allah leaves him to himself. If he selects a faithful and pious woman Allah gives him wealth as well as beauty.
>
> If a woman does not do her duty to her husband she has not done her duty to Allah.

On animal rights:
> If a person kills a sparrow unnecessarily, that sparrow will complain on the Day of Judgement and will say: O Lord! Ask this person as to why he killed me without any reason.

On Jihad (the holy war):
> When Muslim fighters decide to perform jihad, Allah decides to free them from the fire of Hell and when they prepare to undertake a journey for jihad, he takes pride over their existence before the angels and when they take leave of their families, the doors, the walls, and the house weep for them and they become free from sins just as a snake extricates itself from its slough.

… # chapter 3
Shar'iah law

Islamic faith and practice is in reality an introduction to the comprehensive Islamic law. In Islam the difference between law and morals is only marginal. Islamic law has a different function from the laws, regulations and rules we find in the Bible. It is certainly very dissimilar to any modern Western law system. The *Shar'iah* is the most important landmark in Islamic self-knowledge. It is the embodiment of Islam. The law is expressed not only in the beliefs of the Muslim. It is also strongly visible in the *lifestyle* of the true Muslim.

In order to grasp the Islamic self-conception as demonstrated in the Muslims' world mission, attitude towards religious liberty, fundamentalism and terror attacks and the Muslim attitude to conditions in our Western countries, one needs to understand Islamic law. The knowledge of the dynamics, origins, punishments for transgressions and the *modus operandi* of the *Shar'iah*, not only in Islamic countries but also in Muslim homes, is also helpful in this process of understanding the Muslim mind.

Shar'iah law is the element in Islam that a Western person has most difficulty in understanding and accepting. That is especially so in regard to the concepts in the law, the way law and family loyalty are closely linked, and how severe punishments are meted out for transgressions. We have to accept, however, that Western legal systems and the leniency and tolerance shown in our punishing of transgressors are a mystery to many Muslims. The *Shar'iah* law, with its 1,000-year history, is interpreted and applied differently in the various Muslim communities, according to the understanding of the different sects and cultures.

The *Shar'iah*, a comprehensive law system

The word *Shar'iah* is Arabic for 'to introduce, to prescribe'. The word 'path' has the same root. The *Shar'iah* law system is, as mentioned, different from all other law systems in the world. Muslims believe it covers all commands and wishes from Allah, and their salvation depends on their living lives in conformity with the law. Believing in the fundamentality of their law for all mankind, Muslims feel honour bound to make the world their mission.

The comprehensive system of law lays equal emphasis on all aspects relating to the law: rules regarding acts of worship, ritual, acts of murder, rape, theft, and all criminal activities. The law also has detailed rules for trade, property rights and inheritance. The *Shar'iah* is rather detailed in matters that we would classify as belonging to private life and family relations.

The *Shar'iah* has strict rules for worship and rituals in connection with Islam. There are detailed rules for marriage, divorce and unfaithfulness. *Shar'iah* allows a man to have up to four wives. Sexual relationships between unmarried people are condemned. The same law/system takes care of such a variety of matters as drinking alcohol, personal hygiene, table manners, and even how to address a sick person. There are strict rules for women's dress, eating pork, and the punishment for adultery and unfaithfulness in marriage.

There are severe punishments, even execution, for apostasy from Islam.

In comparison, Western laws are divided up into various partly separate areas. We have civil and public laws. Civil law deals with the more personal and family matters. Public law takes care of criminal matters, international affairs and administrative concerns.

The *Shar'iah* law completely dominates the life of the Muslim. It is interesting to notice that *Shar'iah* has a greater place in Islam than theology. Law schools are more important than schools of theology. The *Shar'iah* law is really theology at its strongest in Islam.

Muslims who live among Christians are today experiencing a time of crisis. The issue is the influence of Western thought and secular ideas on the Muslim world. The struggle is between liberals and fundamentalists, modernists and traditionalists. The issue is about how to understand and interpret the *Shar'iah* in the modern world.

The integrated society

In order to appreciate and comprehend the laws in Islam, it must be understood that in Muslim societies and cultural concepts there is no clear dividing line between religion, politics and life in general. In the West we make a distinction between the secular and the spiritual. This difference is not found in Islam. It is not possible for the faithful Muslim to divide life into different categories.

The 'secular' is not separated from the 'holy'. Religion and politics, private and public morals, go together. All aspects of existence are dictated by the divine will of Allah. This will is revealed in the holy writings (the Kor'an) and the law, *Shar'iah*, which is based on and developed from the Kor'an and accepted traditions. It all belongs together like the bricks in a building, with religion as the cement that keeps things in their place. There are no areas in Islamic society and the life of the Muslim that are not affiliated with religion. Allah and life are believed to be inseparable.

Such Christian concepts as 'separation between church and state' and 'give to Caesar what is Caesar's, and to God what is God's' (Matt 22:21) are not to be found in the Islamic world-view. It is in a Christian world-view that various aspects of life are considered as being apart from one another and evaluated according to individual standards.

The Islamic understanding of life has some similarities with the concepts we find in the Old Testament.

The role of law

Generally, Islamic and Western laws are based on similar ethical and moral principles. However, there is a noticeable difference. Western law reflects the will and wishes of the people and thereby defines the rights and duties of men and women in relation to the needs of society. For this reason, transgressors are punished as criminals acting against the social order.

Islamic law, on the other hand, is built on the conviction that the *Shar'iah* is a direct expression of the will of Allah and *his* design for human lives. It is expected that Muslims adapt their lives according to the law without being influenced by the public and private actions of others. Obligations are more important than rights, precisely because the law has its origin in divinity. In this way *Shar'iah* is hardly law in the Western sense. It is a guide to morals and ethics. Legal considerations and the rights of the individual are of secondary importance.

The foundation of Shar'iah law

Islamic law is built on four foundations:

1. The Kor'an is the most important. It is believed to be the infallible revelation from Allah intended for all people in all ages. The Kor'an, however, is not a book of law. As mentioned, only 500 verses (*ayats*) out of more than 6,000 can be applied to legal matters. And these are focused on marriage, inheritance, diet and family life. In reality only 90 *ayats* directly point to legal issues. The rest of the Kor'an contains moral advice that can be used for making laws. And Muslims learned in law were in Islam's early period, as now, experts in interpreting and drawing lessons in these areas.

The kor'anic contributions to *Shar'iah* give the impression, in certain cases, of being somewhat contrived. The reason could be that the prophet, although he claimed divine inspiration, in certain situations seems to have used the words of Allah to defend his own actions and attack personal enemies. For instance, in the Kor'an there is a passage to the effect that an adopted child's legal rights and position in the family do not equal those of the child born into the family by natural birth. This command was 'revealed' to Muhammad at a time when he had to defend his action in marrying his adopted son Zayd's divorced wife. As an adopted child, Zayd was not a real son.

In the same way, the 'revelation' came that false witnesses in a case of adultery should be punished with eighty cuts of a whip. Muhammad received this command at a time when his favourite wife, Aisha, was accused of adultery.

Most Muslims scholars from the various traditions agree that the Kor'an is the divine and primary source of the *Shar'iah*. However, they argue about which parts of the book should be made the foundation for law and also how they should be interpreted.

2. The second source is the *Hadith*. Here we find a rather detailed account of the life of Muhammad. There are stories about where he went, whom he met, what he said and did, what he approved of and condoned, and what he disapproved of and condemned. In the *Hadith* there are also reports about some of the activities and sayings of his companions. In this way the *Hadith* portrays in an interesting way a broad outline and enlightening details of how Islamic principles were lived out. It thereby became a good basis for Islamic law.

The *Hadith*, as one of the secondary sources for the *Shar'iah*, proved to be an area of great contention where the Muslim lawgivers found ample reasons for disagreements. The many *Hadith* collections had accounts that not only differed considerably in content, but the law experts from the various sects also differed in their understanding of the principles for interpretation. There are even accusations that some *Hadiths* were 'fabricated' to give certain controversial laws a basis. There are also examples of cases where the *Hadith* superseded the Kor'an in cases where the Kor'an was not completely clear on an issue, or even when Muhammad in the Kor'an did not show the strictness or harshness the lawmakers wanted.

Two examples are as follows: In *Surah* 11:114 it is recommended that Muslims should have three daily prayer seasons. The *Hadith* abrogates this divine command by suggesting five prayer seasons daily. The *Hadith* recommendation, not the Kor'an command, became one of the Five Pillars of Islam. *Surah* 2: 217 talks about apostasy from Islam, and states that the lives of apostates will not bear fruit in this life or in the coming world. Hell will be their abode. In other words the prophet said that punishment for apostasy would take place after death. The *Hadith* states that the penalty for defection from Islam should be executed in this life. Aisha, Muhammad's last wife, remembered that the prophet once said that there were three reasons for executing a Muslim. They were adultery, murder and apostasy. Also here, unfortunately, the *Hadith* account became the basis for the *Shar'iah*.

3. The third source for Islamic legistration is Ijma. The word means 'Assembly or consensus of opinion'. It was used in connection with *Shar'iah* when the lawgivers could not fully understand the meaning of the Kor'an or the *Hadith*. The ancient legal experts in Islam, however, could not agree on who made up the 'community'. Did it mean all Muslims worldwide or just the scholars?

The debate on the meaning of the word 'consensus' is still present in Islam. Some modern Muslim communities would like to interpret the word *Ijma* to mean that even today there should be the option to reinterpret and rewrite parts of the *Shar'iah* in such a way as to reflect the twenty-first century. There is no doubt that the *Shar'iah* law reflects the social and economic conditions of the Arab Peninsula 1,000 years ago. The principles in the law are not in keeping with modern times and development, even in Muslim countries today.

Nevertheless, Muslim leaders will insist that a law developed in the Arabian Peninsula in the first 300 years of the history of Islam should not be changed. It should be in force because it expressed the will of Allah for all people and at all times.

4. *Qiyas*, meaning measure, scale and analogy, is also a foundation for *Shar'iah* law. *Qiyas* was applied when the lawmakers were not able to find authority in the Kor'an or the

Hadith. Muslims will apply *Qiyas* by drawing conclusions from cases in Islam's history when there is no warrant in the accepted scriptures.

A rather modern case where *Qiyas* has been applied will demonstrate how it is used. The use of tobacco and narcotics is not touched on in any of the Islamic traditional books. Neither the Kor'an nor the *Hadith* has prohibitions against it. This is reasonable. One thousand years ago the use of tobacco was not practised on this side of the Atlantic! Narcotics were not a big problem then either. When it was proven that smoking has ill effects and narcotics became a problem for society, they were put on the same list as alcohol. The use of alcohol is forbidden for Muslims. The *Qiyas* was that when the prophet put alcohol on the list of forbidden things owing to its bad effect on health, he would doubtless have included tobacco and narcotics had they been available in his time. One of the purposes of the divine laws is to serve man's best interest and welfare.

Other influences on the Shar'iah

Muslims will claim that the *Shar'iah* has its roots in Allah's will and wishes for mankind. It is, however, possible to trace other influences on the *Shar'iah* in addition to the four foundations listed. On the Arabian Peninsula there were Jews who lived according to the Mosaic laws from the Old Testament. There were also some Christians who followed the canonical laws of the Eastern traditions. Naturally there were the old tribal laws the Bedouins had developed before Muhammad came on the scene.

As Islam was spread and accepted in various non-Arab countries, some of these local laws were incorporated into the *Shar'iah*. In this way Islamic law became somewhat geared to their cultures.

One of the great problems in the *Shar'iah* is that in criminal cases such as murder, robbery, even adultery and fornication, witnesses are needed before a conviction can be passed. These cases cannot be decided in court on circumstantial evidence. This makes criminal cases extremely difficult to deal with in a *Shar'iah* court. For this reason some Muslim countries have accepted *Shar'iah* laws for civil cases such as inheritance, marriage and family matters, while they have European (Western) laws for criminal cases.

Only a few Islamic countries have accepted *Shar'iah* law completely. Several governments under colonial rule had laws that were a mixture of *Shar'iah* and Western laws. There is, however, a tendency today for more and more countries to introduce Islamic law.

chapter 4

Punishments for transgressions
Religious liberty
Fundamentalism

Punishments for transgressions of the *Shar'iah* are, to some extent, based on the qiyas principle. The word means 'retaliation', 'getting even', 'to attack an enemy's footsteps'.

The penalties for transgressions of Islamic law compared with Western standards appear to be primitive and brutal. Perhaps for that reason very few books are available on the subject in English, and books on Islamic beliefs and practices generally omit this aspect of Islam. This subject, together with the position of women, seems to be an embarrassment to many Muslims. In dealing with this delicate subject we have to generalise, since the punishments differ from country to country and culture to culture.

Specific punishments according to Shar'iah laws

1. *Stoning to death* for adultery (sexual relationship between a married person and partner other than the lawful spouse):
The stoning is to take place where there are no houses or fields. The accusers throw the first stone, then the judge takes part, and finally the witnesses. The body is buried on the same spot and entitled to the usual ablutions and

funeral rites according to Islamic regulations.

2. *Execution* is the punishment for homosexuality.

3. *One hundred stripes* for fornication (sexual relations between two unmarried persons):
There are a number of rules for how and when the flogging can take place. The stick must be without knots; the 100 cuts should not be administered on the same spot on the body. The man should stand; the woman sit down. Wounds inflicted should be only skin deep. The executioner (not a brutal man, rather a scholar in Islamic law) should not use all his force; nor beat so lightly that no harm is done to the offender. Flogging should be avoided in times of intense heat or extreme cold. The flogging of a sick person or nursing mother is not allowed.

4. *Eighty stripes* for false accusations in cases of adultery or fornication.

5. *Execution by the sword* for apostasy (renunciation, abandonment of Islam by word, deed or practice):
Execution by the sword is for the apostate man. In the case of a woman the punishment is imprisonment for life (not all Islamic sects agree on this).

6. *Eighty stripes for a free person, forty for a slave*, for the use of alcohol (includes all kinds of alcoholic beverages):
The accused must be stripped naked to receive the punishment.

7. *Right hand amputated at the joint of the wrist* for theft (there are in Islam detailed laws as to different kinds of theft):
The stump should then be cauterised. For a second theft the right foot should be amputated.

8. *Execution sometimes by crucifixion* for highway robbery and war against the Islamic state.

Surah 5: 33,34:
> *The punishment of those who wage war against Allah and his messenger, and strive with might and main for mischief through the land is: execution, or crucifixion, or the cutting of hands and feet from opposite sides, or exile from the land: That is their disgrace in this world, and a heavy punishment is theirs in the hereafter; except for those who repent before they fall into your power: in that case, know that Allah is oft forgiving, most merciful.*

Some observations

A Western person has a hard time understanding and accepting these harsh methods of punishment. It is obvious that to some extent they are based on principles of revenge and retribution. This, combined with the pain connected with certain corporal punishments, is offputting to the Christian.

Old Testament penalties

Some of the laws in the Old Testament to some extent resemble Muslim practice. The Jews also lived in a society in which the laws had the purpose of promoting public morals, and encouraging the people to be faithful in their religious duties and beliefs. There were laws that governed worship and rituals connected with the temple services. However, there were also divine laws that dealt with murder, sex crimes, treason, perjury and crimes against people and property.

The punishment was also severe, based on a principle from Exodus 21:23-25: *'But if there is a serious injury, you are to take life for life, eye for eye, tooth for tooth, hand for hand, foot for foot, and burn for burn, wound for wound, bruise for bruise.'*

Purpose is prevention

Muslims will defend the severe and often brutal punishments by claiming that they help prevent crimes. Saudi Arabia is one of the countries where the *Shar'iah* in all its details is enforced. The authorities point out that their country has the lowest crime rate in the world. The severe punishments serve to deter others. A young Saudi told me that when he was a small boy his father took him to the local mosque where some chopped-off hands were hanging from the branches of a tree. It made a great impression on the boy, and he decided that he was not going to be a thief!

The punishment also serves to guard morals and chastity.

It is, however, a fact that Saudi Arabian courts usually hold their cases behind closed doors where there is no access for the press, and there is heavy censorship on all newspapers. There are even stories reporting that news releases are doctored to fit in with the claims of high morals.

Mitigating circumstances

The severe punishments have to some extent to be balanced with certain humane elements when Muslim magistrates, according to *Shar'iah*, take into consideration the circumstances of the crimes. There is room for human weaknesses, and allowance is made for things such as 'periodic insanity' and even 'irresistible temptations'. To this must be added the strict rules for approval of the reliability of the witnesses in each case. There are heavy punishments for people who commit perjury.

We should bear in mind that, by comparison with Western law, Islamic laws are more focused on the individual. In Muslim courtrooms there is the possibility of the accuser setting the criminal free by forgiving the crime or accepting blood money or compensation. A father is able to free a man accused of the rape of his daughter by throwing his coat over the criminal the moment he has his head on the block.

It is interesting that in some cases of theft the stolen items can be a mitigating circumstance. Amputation for stealing is not incurred when alcohol, guitars, crucifixes, or chessboards have been stolen. It is forbidden to own and use these items. They are not only useless to the owner; they are a danger to his spiritual life.

Primitive societies and severe punishments

As mentioned, *Shar'iah* laws have a thousand-year history. They came into existence after the age Muhammad characterised as 'the Time of Ignorance'. They were put together after long periods of primitive living, barbaric conditions and low morals among the people on the Arabian Peninsula, at a time when most Arabs were illiterate.

Is there a case for accepting that people living in such backward conditions needed detailed rules and laws to regulate their lives? Is it also reasonable to accept that people living under those conditions needed harsh punishments as warnings against severe violations? *Shar'iah* law meets these two conditions, making clear not only what is forbidden but also what is allowed.

The author of this book, when a guest of a paramount chief in West Africa, witnessed a court case in which seven men were accused of having murdered a young virgin and, in a ritual meal, eaten her kidneys. They believed that such an act would secure them political power and influence in the tribal hierarchy. All seven were sentenced to death by hanging, and the judges recommended that the hangings should take place in the centre of their villages – with times and places announced and all officials required to be present. Later I had the opportunity to voice my concern about the public hangings to my friend, the paramount chief. He said that we had to understand that the men condemned to death came from a primitive background, had no education whatsoever and lived in deprived areas. Their fellow tribesmen would understand the severity of the crime only when they personally witnessed the hangings.

Is one of the reasons for the austerity of the punishments in Islamic law to be found in their historic foundation, as they were formulated in the Times of Ignorance when people were quite backward?

This could, of course, mean that in developed Islamic countries today there should be leniency in the penalties to fit modern times. Such a change in penalties, however, would be difficult, as the mullahs believe that the laws, with their roots in the Kor'an and *Hadith*, cannot be changed. They were designed by Allah for all people in all places and at all times.

On the basis of the harshness of penalties in Islam we can better appreciate the amazement with which Muslims view our comparatively light sentences, humane penalty systems and tolerable living conditions in our prisons.

The concept of religious liberty in Islam

In connection with Islamic laws and the negative feelings they provoke in the Western mind, as far as their demands and punishments are concerned, we will briefly touch upon the question of religious liberty – or lack of it – in Muslim lands. We have great difficulty in accepting their attitude in this area. We think that the Muslim is unreasonable and illogical in the important area of religious liberty. There are cases where Muslim girls in France demand the right to wear the *hijab* (veil) in the classroom, while Christians in the country they came from were not permitted to have their own schools.

In some Scandinavian countries Muslims not only expect the authorities to supply them with building plots and pay for the buildings, but even to pay the expenses connected with the running of Kor'anic schools, mosques and centres for the propagation of Islam. At the same time we have news that a woman from a Scandinavian country was expelled from a Muslim country because she distributed Christian literature.

Muslims have a tendency to demand full religious liberty in countries where they are in the minority. This claim includes the right to build mosques, keep their prayer schedules even in the middle of working hours, to circumcise their daughters in certain Islamic cultures, and to be allowed to apply *Shar'iah* law in family affairs when their women have connections with non-Muslim (Christian) men – the last resulting in the terrible 'execution for the sake of keeping the family honour'. There is also a call for permission to apply Islamic law when dealing with the apostates who turn to Christianity.

These requests, rightly when they are against our laws, are not met. In some cases, however, Muslims will take matters into their own hands and execute their daughters and get rid of apostates from Islam. In such cases they have to face our courts and be punished according to our laws. In these situations, however, when Western courts penalise Muslims for following *Shar'iah* law, those punished become 'martyrs for the sake of Islam'. All of which could give the impression that Muslims are unreasonable, even dishonest.

It is hard for a Western person to understand their position.

Let us try to view the situation from the Muslim side. The key concept is that everything is integrated; there are no borders between the religious and the secular. Where religion, law, government and private life are inseparable, religious freedom is a preposterous idea. This concept is strongly enhanced when you believe that Islam is the only unadulterated and irrefutable religion, Muhammad the last authentic prophet, *Shar'iah* law the only valid law. Such an impetus will make any truly believing Muslim fight for his rights in situations where he is in a minority. At the same time such convictions in areas where Islam has the controlling authority ensure that no heresy such as Christianity is tolerated to disturb Muslim religious life and beliefs.

Islamic fundamentalism

Fundamentalism is a global problem. For our purpose we will define fundamentalism as:

A strong and detailed adherence to orthodox beliefs that has developed into an aggressive resistance to everything in society which is regarded as being in conflict with the holy writings accepted by the fundamentalist.

Fundamentalism and fundamentalists are more visible today than ever before. They are to be found among all religions, including Christianity, Hinduism and Judaism. Perhaps Muslim fundamentalists are more visible than their counterparts in other religions because Islamic fanaticism is often expressed in murderous acts. Islamic fanaticism focuses on the unity and sovereignty of Allah, the divine origin of the Kor'an, the final prophethood of Muhammad and the blind obedience to Islamic laws and traditions. Their fight is to establish the earthly kingdom of Allah where religion and government are completely integrated, and where Islam is the only religion with no regard or tolerance of other religions.

Islamic fundamentalism is a reaction against modernism and the Western (secular) influence on Muslim societies. Muslim fundamentalists find their justification for existence in a one-sided and rather biased interpretation of the Kor'an and the Hadiths. Their message is not only turned against non-Muslims, but also against fellow Muslims who they think are not living up to the ideal standard in Islam or even those whose concepts of their faith do not meet those of the fundamentalists.

As they see it, the solution to the multiple problems Islam is facing today is: 'We have left the old true teaching and the path of the pioneers. For that reason we no longer enjoy the blessing of Allah. We must return to and obey the old religion that was practised by Muhammad and his companions.'

Not all Muslims approve of this radical variety of Islam. Many want to live in peace and toleration. However, under pressure they are inclined to support the radical position and the fight for so-called 'reform ideas'. Their Islamic upbringing and peer pressure force them to take a stand for something they would rather be without.

Christian traditions of all kinds are also exposed to fundamentalism and its extreme preaching and activities. However, their fight is usually confined to the spoken or written word. Still there are crude examples where 'Christians' have used arms in defence of themselves or on people of different persuasions.

chapter 5

The Five Pillars

According to a *Hadith*, the archangel Gabriel visited Muhammad and asked him, *'What is Islam?'* Muhammad's reply was that to be a Muslim was to accept the five obligations named the Five Pillars of Islam. They embrace the confession of faith, the prayers, and the fast, the distribution of alms, and the pilgrimage to Mecca. Next the angel asked the prophet, *'What is faith?'* The answer was belief in Allah, his angels, his books, his messengers and the day of judgement.

The Five Pillars

It is expected that each Muslim will strictly adhere to five visible expressions of the Islamic religion. There are reasons why there are exemptions from observing the creed. These exemptions are allowed when conditions, climate or circumstances created by men make observance impossible or difficult. However, a good and faithful Muslim is expected to conform to the five pillars.

1. The confession of faith (*Shahada*)

'I bear witness that there is no god but Allah, and that Muhammad is the messenger of Allah.' This is known as the *Shahada* (meaning *to witness*), consisting of two statements, a combination of various texts from the Kor'an

which Muslims are expected to declare and believe.

The name of the divinity, Allah, is tied in with the human messenger, Muhammad. Had the *Shahada* only said, 'There is only one god, that is Allah,' Jews and Christians could have claimed that it was also their belief. In order to make sure people understood that Muhammad founded a new religion, or a distinct reform-movement, the earthly prophet had to link his name with divinity.

We have to some extent applied the same principle when various Christian traditions wanted to emphasise their differences. We talk about Lutherans, Calvinists, and Wesleyans all connecting *their* churches with the names of the earthly founders. But these differences are accepted. They are still Christians.

Muhammad wanted to make sure that the ordinary Arab in his day would know where to find the true faith. And that was wherever Allah was proclaimed as one god and the faith explained by Muhammad. Muslims all over the world, irrespective of language and race, will many times daily declare their faith in these two statements *in Arabic.*

The *Shahada* is whispered into the ear of the newborn baby. These are the last words a dying Muslim should hear. The *Shahada* is said as the grace at the table, at circumcision, at weddings, when believers are called to prayer, and when soldiers are ready for war. The *Shahada* is the yardstick and measuring rod for Muslims. It must be said aloud, in Arabic, and in front of witnesses. *Tawhid*, the word for Allah's unity, indivisibility, absoluteness and only reality is the most important creed in Islam. It is Islam's greatest proclamation.

2. The ritual prayers (*Salah*)

Salah means worship and prayer. Muslims are called to

prayer five times daily, in the morning, at noon, late afternoon, just after sunset and later in the evening.

Theologians have with great exactness calculated the hours and minutes for the times of prayers in the entire world. There are strict rules for the prayers, and only Muslims can take part. Before they do so they must have cleaned their clothes and bodies, even the places where they pray, and must face the holy city of Mecca in Saudi Arabia.

There are two forms of ablutions. The greater includes the washing of the whole body. This should, for instance, be done after bleeding, intercourse, childbirth, touching a corpse, etc. The lesser ablution includes the washing of hands, feet and face, and is applied when a person has slept, been to the toilet, been bitten by an insect or touched a dog. When no water is available, sand, earth and even a stone can be used for the ablution, no doubt a sensible rule in a religion that was developed in a desert area. The ritual washing, a prerequisite for taking part in the prayers, is a symbolic cleansing that frees the worshipper from the above-mentioned physical impurities.

Impurities on the religious, spiritual and psychological level such as lust, lying, stealing, losing one's temper, backbiting, hate or envy are not mentioned as reasons for ablution. The main reasons are somewhat similar to the attitude of Jewish people. When the physical side is clean it is sufficient.

In Matthew chapter 5 we find that, six times, Jesus draws attention to the fact that is it not only murder but also anger that is condemned; not only adultery but also lust. Love for their enemies is required of his followers. This is expressed in the ablution rituals in the New Testament. Baptism is 'not a removal of dirt from the body but a pledge of a good conscience towards God' (1 Peter 3:21).

It is also affirmed in the foot washing at the last supper, when Jesus said to Peter, 'Unless I wash you, you have no part with me.' (John 13:1-10.) A symbolic cleansing with water in Christianity is not only from the physical stains of sin; together with faith, the ceremony also cleanses the motives, inclinations and guilt feelings that transgressions cause.

A human voice calls the faithful to prayer from the minarets. The call to prayer and the prayers themselves are in Arabic. The Friday prayer is special. It is followed by a sermon. An *imam (mullah, sheikh)* leads out in the daily prayers. Islam has no employed and salaried priesthood. It is primarily a lay-movement. The exception is in the greater mosques with many worshippers. They employ men of learning in law and theology to be in charge. In the smaller congregations it is generally the person who has the best knowledge of Arabic who is the prayer-leader. Only one out of seven Muslims has Arabic as his or her native language. Women pray separately from men. A woman cannot be a prayer-leader if there is one man present in the praying community.

The prayers are completely ritualistic. All who take part whisper the same words and go through the same movements simultaneously. *Rak'ah*, with its root in the Arabic word 'to bend down', includes in the prayer situation regular words and movements repeated constantly. One *Rak'ah* consists of a standing position, a bow, a prostration and a seated position and then finally a standing position. Each prayer has several *Rak'ahs*. Certain sentences in the prayer are repeated 17 times, some phrases 450 times, and the forehead will touch the ground 34 times each day during the five prayer seasons.

Private prayers, so important with Christians, also have a

place in Islam. However, they are not equal to the ritual prayers said in public. The private petitions are uttered generally in a whisper after the ritual prayer. Often in the personal prayers one of the 99 names of Allah is applied. It is the name that is most applicable to the request of the petitioner. If a Muslim prays for healing, the name that describes Allah as the Healer is used.

The prayer is directed towards Mecca, which is shown by a niche in the wall of the mosque opposite the entrance. Whenever a person enters a mosque, he or she is walking in the direction of Mecca. When a Muslim is in an area where there are no mosques, he should find the direction of Mecca, spread out his mat and pray at the appropriate times.

3. Social Taxation *(Zak'ah)*

Zak'ah is the Third Pillar in Islam. The word means 'purify'. *Zak'ah* is to give up to a worthy cause a portion of what one owns or earns. This financial sacrifice will 'purify' or legitimise what is left for one's own use. *Zak'ah* is not necessarily a tax paid, although some Muslim governments put that amount on top of the regular tax. It is used to help the poor, debtors, new Muslims and people who fight for the cause of Islam, to liberate slaves and also to pay the *Zak'ah* collectors. The alms cannot be used for mosque building nor to support the *Zak'ah* payer's own family.

The amount is usually 2.5% of income. However, it varies according to how a person makes a living. There are detailed rules according to whether the income is a fixed salary, in livestock, trade or industry. In working out how the *Zak'ah* principle is practically applied to various income groups, Muslim scholars also reveal the tremendous — somewhat legalistic — emphasis there exists in Islam. For instance, the *Zak'ah* for a farmer in Egypt is 2.5% while the farmer in Uganda should pay 5%. The difference between the two Muslim farmers is that the Egyptian, in order to get a harvest, has to irrigate his fields, while his Ugandan counterpart has the rain sent over his farm directly from Allah.

In addition to the *Zak'ah* the Muslim is also encouraged to pay a *Sadaqah*, a voluntary giving of alms. The *Sadaqah* is used for welfare purposes. As *Zak'ah* is one of the Five Pillars, the paying of it is also a part of Islamic worship.

4. The fast *(Sawm)*

The official fast takes place in *Ramadan*, the ninth month in the Muslim calendar. It is a yearly event lasting four weeks. In addition to the *Ramadan* fast there are also freewill days of fasting that serve as penance for transgression of an Islamic rule, or a personal reason why one wants to abstain from food and drink.

During *Ramadan* a Muslim should not eat, drink, smoke or have sexual intercourse between sunrise and sunset. It is also recommended that Muslims abstain from listening to music or indulging in any other activity that pleases the senses and enhances the desires.

According to Islamic traditions the Kor'an was revealed to Muhammad in the last ten days of the ninth month, the *Ramadan* month. For that reason it is recommended that Muslims read the whole Kor'an during the fast.

Islamic scholars cannot give a precise reason for the importance of the *Sawm*. The fast itself is of benefit for the body. It can in this way also be a cleansing of the soul and a help in fighting against selfishness. The fact that all Muslims worldwide take part in the *Ramadan* at the same time helps them to cherish a bond of fellowship with other Muslims, to feel they are part of a world community, and also identify with the poor and hungry, of whom there are many in the Islamic world.

In the detailed regulations for the fast we find, as in other Islamic rituals, rules for what is allowed and what is forbidden during the 28-29 days of fasting. It is, for instance, not permitted to inhale dust or smoke, to dive, to have a bath or cause oneself to vomit. However, also in *Ramadan* we find the interesting and fascinating exemptions or dispensations that are so typical of Islam. They help to give the impression that Islam is a humane religion, even when there are requirements that seem rather inhumane. For example, it is not required to keep the fast when you are travelling, pregnant, or a minor. It is recommended that children fast for half the day.

With its four weeks of fasting during daylight, *Ramadan* is believed to have a positive effect on health. Regular fasts, when they are not excessive and are kept within the rules, have a health-promoting value. This positive effect, however, is lost if families indulge in immense meals after sunset.

There is nevertheless one aspect of the fast that is certainly *not* in agreement with healthful living. It is forbidden during the daylight hours to drink any form of fluid. This causes serious problems in the tropics or subtropics. There have been complaints from police in Muslim countries that there is more crime during the month of *Ramadan* than any other month of the year.

The Kor'an and Islam had their cradle in an area where the day and night hours were of equal length. The religion divided the day accordingly. Twelve hours of fasting is no big deal. As time passed, however, Islam was accepted by people living in other latitudes with short days in the winter and longer days in the summertime. In the most Northern part of Norway a Muslim immigrant said that north of the Arctic Circle a Muslim could eat day and night when the *Ramadan* fell in the winter. However, eighteen years later, when it fell in the summer, he could not eat at all for 28-29 days. The Muslim calendar, following the cycle of the moon, is ten days shorter than our Gregorian calendar so its months gradually move round the astronomical year. For example, in AD2000 the Islamic year began on 6 April and Ramadam on 27 November; in AD2003 the year began on 5 March and Ramadam on 27 October. Theologians in Mecca suggested that they followed Mecca fasting time, and thus solved the problem in Northern Norway.

It is claimed that the Kor'an existed from eternity and was sent by Allah to Muhammad. Hence some Christians ask Muslims whether in their belief system the creator of the universe did not realise that the length of days is not the same on a round globe or that Islam would eventually have followers in all geographical areas.

5. The pilgrimage *(Hajj)*
Al-Hajj, which has the great pilgrimage to Mecca as its goal, is obligatory for all Muslims once in a lifetime. Again here we have interesting and humane exceptions. A person who is not in good health and is too poor to pay the fare to Mecca is not expected to make the pilgrimage. A person must be without debt before he travels to Mecca, and at the same time must leave sufficient funds to sustain the family in his absence. The pilgrim should be in possession of a round-trip ticket to Jeddah, which is the nearest airport and seaport to Mecca.

Only Muslims belonging to a branch of Islam that is accepted by the leaders in Saudi Arabia have access to Mecca, the holy city. A few miles before Mecca is reached by car or bus, there are not only signs telling non-Muslims to take another road; there are also police checkpoints examining the papers of all persons in the vehicles. The Muslim authorities try to ensure that no 'infidel' enters the holy city.

When a person does not have health and strength to travel to Mecca and take part in the one week's strenuous exercises connected with the pilgrimage, he or she can do it by substitute. Women can take part only when a male, who must be a near relative either by birth or marriage, accompanies them. The *Hajj* occurs in the twelfth month of the Islamic calendar. All activities take place in Mecca and the nearest neighbourhood, with the *Ka'bah* as the centre. The programme is a six-day venture, but is often prolonged with a trip to Medina, the next most sacred city in Islam.

The *Hajj* begins with some dedication ceremonies, comprising the greater ablution, and then the person dresses up in the *ihram*, the special white pilgrimage dress that is worn throughout the event. In this way the Muslim will be in the '*ihram* state of consecration'. The *Hajj* also consists of many rituals that have to be performed in the right order and the right place in and around Mecca. Each step demonstrates a belief in Allah and respect for the prophet Muhammad. The ceremonies also bring to mind Abraham, Ishmael and Hagar as well as the history and heritage of Islam.

It all begins in the elaborate mosque in Mecca with a visit to the *Ka'bah* and the black stone. According to tradition this stone was sent by Allah and dropped down from heaven. One of the companions of Muhammad, the second khalif Omar, after the death of the prophet, said as he kissed the stone: 'I know you are only a stone with power to do neither good nor bad. If I had not seen the prophet kiss you, I would not have done it.'

The next step is to walk the four miles to Minna where

the pilgrims pray and meditate. The following day the trip will continue to Mount Arafat, where they stand for up to eight hours to focus their thinking on Muhammad and his life. This part of the pilgrimage is a reminder of the day of judgement. It was at Mount Arafat that the prophet preached his last sermon in 632. The Arafat experience is the high point, not only in the *Hajj* but also in the Muslim's spiritual experience. From there the pilgrims return to Mecca. On the way they pass Minna, where they stone three pillars symbolising Satan. Muslims believe that on this spot Abraham was tempted to sacrifice Ishmael (not Isaac as the Bible tells us). Symbolically, Muslims at Minna throw stones at the evil one and his works. Some of the wealthier Muslims will sacrifice a goat, sheep, cow or camel, and the meat is distributed to the poor. Then the pilgrims walk back to Mecca, where they again walk round the *Ka'bah*, kiss the black stone, and visit places in Mecca important in the history of Islam.

The pilgrims then take the title *Al-Hajji* and are honoured upon their return home. In some cases they will even dye their hair pink and wear a white skullcap.

The pilgrimage to Mecca is regarded as the culmination of a Muslim's spiritual life and experience. On this occasion the history and inheritance of Islam come alive. The places where Muhammad and his companions lived are visited. It is also an opportunity to meet Muslims from the whole Islamic world on equal terms. There prevails a feeling of unity that surpasses racial, age, linguistic, and social differences. This elevating experience is combined with a feeling of having been cleansed from transgressions against the will of Allah, even a belief that Muhammad is a personal intercessor with Allah.

In the Time of Ignorance Mecca, the *Ka'bah* and the

black stone were the places where the scattered idol-worshipping Bedouin tribes travelled for their pilgrimage. Today Mecca is the centre of worship for 1.2 billion Muslims. More than 2 million of the faithful visit the city each year.

It is obvious that the *Hajj* is patterned after the Feast of Tabernacles described in Leviticus 23:33-36. That Jewish festival was instituted 2,000 years before Muhammad came on the scene. The rituals are conspicuously similar.

Psychologically, all religions use pilgrimages for spiritual edification. The experiences of travelling, meeting other people, and receiving new impressions render inspiration.

Jihad, the holy war

There are Muslim theologians who claim the *Jihad* should be the Sixth Pillar in Islam. The root of the word *Jihad* means 'effort' and 'struggle' in the name of, or for, religion. It can be interpreted to mean a divine call to a war to spread Islam to non-Muslim territories, or to defend Islam against dangers and threats. The terrorist organisations that have been active in the USA and Israel will vouch for this aggressive interpretation of the word *Jihad*.

Today the concept of *Jihad* — the conditions for involvement and how the holy war itself is conducted — is a controversial subject. In a *literal* war, where the fight is for the Islamic cause, only men can take part. Furthermore, it is stated that the war should not be conducted against fellow Muslims, and those who are killed in the *Jihad* are martyrs who will ascend straight to paradise.

Jihad, according to the Kor'an and *Hadith*, can also mean that a Muslim is engaged in a worthy cause; for instance, campaigns against narcotics, alcohol, tobacco, pollution, pornography, underdevelopment, illiteracy and other causes. Peace-loving Muslims will prefer this positive interpretation of the word.

Some Christians today use the word 'crusade' when they speak about fights against alcohol and tobacco. We have to understand that in the same way that the word *Jihad* has a negative connotation for Christians, the word *crusade* reminds the Muslims of the unjustified attacks on Muslims more than 900 years ago.

Religion enhanced by body movements

All the five (perhaps six) pillars in Islam are connected with rituals in which the worshipper is personally, and to a great extent, physically involved. In Christianity the religious specialists who are consecrated and professionally trained for the task generally perform the ceremonies. The audiences are in many cases passive spectators, watching what is going on for their benefit. Hopefully, the audience will have its attention and thoughts focused on the deeper meaning of the rituals and the possible effect obtained by the ceremony. In Islam, all present take an active part in the ritualistic services.

In the *Shahadah* the two sentences, 'There is no god but Allah,' and 'Muhammad is the messenger of Allah,' are said aloud by all worshippers. The prayer is the pillar with most movements and rituals. An ablution is expected, the direction to Mecca has to be found, and the motions connected with the *Ra'ka*, from the standing to the prostrate position on the prayer mat, can be physically demanding. It is recommended that the *Zak'ah* be paid personally to a worthy cause or a poor person. The Fast demands that Muslims neither eat nor drink during daylight hours and that at least once in a lifetime they make the pilgrimage to Mecca (including a 25-mile walk to Mount Arafat, which includes various activities lasting six days).

There is a high percentage of illiterate people in parts of the Muslim world. Consequently, many followers of Islam are not able, by word or logic, to explain what they believe. However, adherence to the Five Pillars, where beliefs are also expressed with body movements, is probably one of the reasons why so many cling to a religion they can neither explain nor defend. In their daily lives their faith is expressed in reflex movements of their bodies.

One thousand four hundred years ago it must also have been a huge task to explain the differences among the three Abrahamic, monotheistic religions that, in spite of their doctrinal differences, all called God by the name Allah. (Christian missions have the same problem today.) The founders of Islam were far-seeing when they introduced into their religious rituals marked differences which distinguished Islam from Judaism and Christianity. Especially in the prayer ceremonies is this obvious:

* Some of the Christians prayed facing the East, and the Jews turned their faces towards Jerusalem. Muhammad told the people to pray towards Mecca.

* Christians were summoned to church by a bell. The Jews used the ram's horn. Muhammad introduced the call to the mosque by the male voice.

* Christians on the Arabian Peninsula worshipped on Sunday and the Jews on Sabbath (Saturday). Muhammad made Friday the day for prayer.

* Christians were encouraged to pray twice a day (morning and evening) and the Jews three times a day (morning, noon and evening). The *Hadith* told the Muslims to pray five times daily.

chapter 6

The Five Articles of Faith

In Islam there are Five of Faith.

Among the world religions only Christianity had articles of faith. The non-Christian religions expressed their beliefs in the way they worshipped, and in their ethics and lifestyles, philosophy and mysticism. Although they had holy books, these did not systematically and briefly outline the religious teaching and belief system. As Christianity involved itself in foreign missions, including attempts to win over people from other religious traditions, it became necessary to express what they believed and stood for in a few simple sentences. These creeds generally listed the most important beliefs the adherents were expected to follow. The formation of creeds was not only helpful in meeting the needs of Christian missionaries, but also in taking care of heresies within their own ranks.

A legalistic religion, Islam enables followers to perform their duties by providing them with a detailed model for worship in the Five Pillars. The Five Articles are therefore an expression of the Islamic theology and faith.

1. The doctrine of Allah

The word Islam means 'surrender' to the will of Allah. Allah is the only god. His unity and indivisibility is the most important article of faith in Islam. No human language can define or describe Allah. No one is like him. Only he is worthy of being worshipped. Allah is active as creator and sustainer, lifegiver and the one who takes life away. Only he controls his creation.

Allah has 99 names. However, the names do not divide Allah, who is one. The names express his many attributes. Allah is merciful and benevolent. All *Surahs* except one begin with the words: 'In the name of Allah. Most gracious, most merciful. He has all power and is not challenged by anyone or anything. He is wisdom itself and knows happenings in the past, present and future. Allah is eternal; he has neither beginning nor end. Time, space or circumstances do not limit him.'

Islam makes it clear that Allah has no partners — son, father, brother, wife, sister or daughter.

A study of the 99 names renders an insight into the Muslim's perception of Allah, how he functions and the place of religion in life. There are three names and qualities Christians attribute to God that have great importance in the Christian concept of God's character and being. These are missing in Islam and not found among the 99 names. In the Bible, God is Father, Son and Spirit. These divine identities, so important for the Christian, are not applied to Allah by the Muslims.

There is, no doubt, some significant overlapping between the Allah of Islam and the God of the Christians. It is, however, interesting to notice that God for the Christian believer is perceived to be loving and caring. Omnipotence is also revealed in humility and gentleness. The Allah of Islam and the 99 names describing his character have connotations of power and control, even retribution. The sovereignty of Allah is stressed as being of a political and military nature.

The words in the Kor'an on Allah's greatness seem also to be based on a principle like the Old Testament 'eye for eye and tooth for tooth'. The teachings of the Bible in the New Testament are more of the 'turning the other cheek' principle.

To this must be added the very significant idea that when a Christian thinks and talks about his or her God the concept includes the Trinity: Father, Son and Holy Spirit. To the Muslim this is blasphemy and understood as polytheism. It is interpreted to mean that the Christians worship *three* gods. Among Muslims it is even conceived that the Trinity consists of God the father, Mary the mother, and Jesus as son. It is taken for granted that where there are father and son there must also be a mother. In this way the Christian God is understood as being immoral.

2. The doctrine of the Angels

Christians and Muslims share a belief in the existence of angels. The Islamic understanding is somewhat different from the Christian concept, although there are marked similarities and there is some overlapping. It is worth noticing that the doctrine on angels is mentioned second in the Articles of Faith in Islam. This indicates, no doubt, the role these supernatural beings play in the heavenly hierarchy.

Angels are created from light and have intelligence and the ability to speak, think, see and listen. They do not possess a free will and are, therefore, not able to disobey the commands or go against the will of Allah. They are completely loyal to his wishes. Their main tasks are worship and service. They are the administrators of Allah's universe and protectors of faithful Muslims, have a part in executing the judgement of Allah, and serve as his messengers. In this way each angel has a special position and assignment. Gabriel is one of four archangels. His special, particular mission is to reveal Allah's will and plans to the prophets. Another archangel is Israfil, proclaiming among other things the resurrection. Other prominent angels are Izrail, the angel of death, Malik who commands hell, and Radwan who is in charge of paradise.

Two angels, one at the right side who makes a register of all good deeds, and one at the left side who writes down the evil acts, accompany each person. On the day of judgement each person will face these accounts. There will be no denial of their accuracy.

The outstanding position angels possess in Islamic understanding is due to the fact that, at the time of Muhammad, there was widespread belief in legions of invisible beings, gods and demigods, which people feared and worshipped. By Muhammad's stressing that all these supernatural creatures – including the angels – were completely subject to Allah's will and wishes, Allah, the supreme being, was portrayed as the unique one who ruled and had dominion. There was no one beside him. All the others depended on him for authority and the ability to act.

The Jinn

The *jinn* are also intelligent beings created by Allah. From the Arabic word *jinni* we get the word genius. The *jinn* are created from smokeless fire, and angels from light, while men and women were formed from clay. There are two kinds of *jinn*. Some have human natures, others are incorporeal. The 'human' *jinn* are religious. Once, Muhammad met some of these, and they were converted to Islam. On that occasion a mosque was built in Mecca named the Mosque of the *Jinn*.

Some *jinn* are friendly, even helpful. Others are hostile

and wicked. Some are pretty and attractive, while others are hideous and ugly. Their lifespan is longer than that of human beings. Some living today were contemporary with Muhammad. *Jinn* assisted Solomon in building the Temple in Jerusalem.

Iblis, Satan, was originally an angel. According to Islamic tradition, Allah assigned him the task of tempting human beings. Other Muslim traditions claim that Iblis lost his angelic nature by disobeying Allah and was transformed into a *jinni*. As such he tempts people to transgress the will and commands of Allah. This explanation is closest to the biblical explanation. Muslims have a problem with this, though. At least one angel had to have free will.

3. Revealed Scriptures

Christianity is a revealed religion. That means that divinity has taken the initiative in making the ultimate known to man. In Christianity this took place when Jesus Christ was born among men. The incarnation was made plain in the Bible. A belief in the guidance of Allah in the lives of Muslims is revealed in Islamic writings, the Kor'an, and further developed in the *Hadith*. Muslims accept earlier recorded scriptures such as the *Torah* (Jewish religious law and learning), the Psalms of David and the gospel about Jesus. However, they believe that the Jews and Christians have distorted these scriptures. For that reason they believe that the Bible cannot be trusted. Therefore they believe that Allah sent Gabriel to Muhammad with the unadulterated message from heaven.

The Kor'an is the last and final revelation and authority sent from Allah to mankind. It was revealed to Muhammad, the last prophet and founder of Islam, the universal religion.

Muslims also believe that prophets appeared on the

scene before Muhammad. They were, however, 'local' in the sense that they were sent to particular tribes and people-groups. Muhammad, they believe, was a *global* prophet, sent with a book to all people.

4. The Messengers of Allah

The Arabic word for prophet, *Nabi*, is not confined to a person who foretells future events. It has the meaning, rather, of one who is close to Allah by being completely dedicated to him. This intimate relationship makes him worthy of being the recipient of Allah's messages. These divine revelations are entrusted to the people in the form of scriptures which show how to live here and how to find the way to paradise.

There is another Arabic word for prophet. In the Shahada, Muhammad is called *Rasul*. Both words can also mean messenger or apostle. In Islamic understanding, a prophet is a person who is without blame and irreproachable in character and actions from the moment Allah has called him.

The Kor'an names 28 prophets. Of these, 21 are mentioned in the Bible, 18 in the Old Testament and three (Jesus, John the Baptist and Zachariah) in the New Testament. There are many other biblical persons mentioned in the Kor'an. Only four of the prophets in the Kor'an are Arabs. Interestingly, one of the named prophets is Alexander the Great. It is maintained that many hundreds of years before the advent of Muhammad, Alexander, by his military campaigns, paved the way for Islam. Perhaps that is why he is so honoured!

The *Hadith* (Islamic prophetic traditions) mentions that 124,000 prophets *(nabi)* throughout the ages have been sent by Allah to humankind.

As mentioned, the Kor'an emphasises that Muhammad

is the last messenger sent by Allah, so having the seal of the prophetic office. After Muhammad, anyone claiming to be a prophet sent by Allah is a deceiver and will be punished accordingly.

5. Last events and the day of judgement

The belief and teaching about what happens after death, at the end of history, matters concerning the day of judgement, the resurrection of the body, paradise and hell, are joined together in one meaningful and important article of faith in Islam. The teachings about the last events have a significant role to play in the Kor'an. One day, known only and decided by Allah, the world will be annihilated in a comprehensive catastrophe of nature. On that day the bodies of all who have died will be united with their souls, while those who are alive will die and then go through the same experience, thereby joining the group. Then all who have ever lived are summoned in front of Allah's throne, alone and helpless, the way they were born into the world. The time has come for each person to give an account of his life and actions.

People, *jinn*, even animals, will face the judge and judgement. Those who have rejected the commands and decrees of Allah – that is those who discarded the teachings of Islam – will be sent to a terrible and ghastly place, hell. There they will be separated from Allah and will be in a state of torment from which they will find no relief. The Islamic hell consists of fire, black smoke and what follows from such conditions. There are unnumbered descriptions that paint the sufferings of the Muslim hell in the most horrifying details, but Muslim scholars do not approve of all of them. On the other hand, those who have believed in, trusted and followed Allah's commands will enter a life of happiness.

Paradise is a place with shade, water in abundance and streams of wine. The Kor'an even promises that there one will be dressed in silk and will wed black-eyed virgins (*Sura* 44: 53-54).

It is interesting that the Kor'an depicts Paradise as a place where the Bedouins will attain the desires and comforts that they missed in their experience in desert life. The Muslim Paradise has – perhaps a little sarcastically – been described as a 'glorified night club'. Although the hereafter in Islam, with all its comforts and pleasures, is often portrayed in rather improper details, it should be mentioned that not all Muslim theologians accept the various interpretations and descriptions.

Predestination, the will of Allah

As some Muslims claim that the *Jihad* is a sixth pillar of Islam, many Muslims claim that there is a sixth article of faith. This article is predestination, and founded on the fact that Allah is not only the creator but also the maintainer. With these attributes not only does he cause *everything* that happens on earth, but it is all part of his eternal purpose.

The belief that everything that happens on earth is predestined assures the Muslim that his fate is in the hands of Allah, which gives him certainty, confidence and peace. It gives him the conviction that whatever happens to him, even severe trials, is in accordance with the will of the almighty, the omniscient but also the merciful.

This belief that Allah has foreordained all things is best expressed in the word *'insha'llah'*, used by the Muslim whenever he talks about something he is going to do in the future. The meaning is 'if Allah wills'. It is based on *Sura* 18:24-25, and the words express the dependence of the human will on Allah's will.

However, this doctrine that Allah has predetermined all things has a somewhat negative effect on Muslim society. Why work hard, be educated, and have goals in life, when one in reality has no influence on one's development? In this doctrine, no doubt misunderstood by many Muslims, one can perhaps find the reason why Muslim countries generally are among the least developed in the world. Children attending schools in Islamic areas are on average few.

chapter 7

The Muslim's Lifestyle

The most visible expression of the Islamic faith is its obedience to the Five Pillars. Among these, the ritual prayers and the fast strike one especially. They have become a kind of trademark for Islam. When outsiders talk about Muslims, these two pillars are the first to be mentioned. However, obedience to the Islamic law, the *Shar'iah* with its detailed admonitions, counsels, prohibitions and the threat of the harsh punishments for transgressions, is the overshadowing factor in the life of the Muslim from cradle to grave.

Childhood, youth, puberty and circumcision

The first words a newborn baby will hear are from the *Shahada*: 'There is no god but Allah. Muhammad is the prophet of Allah.' In many Muslim cultures the child is named on the seventh day after birth. In some cases an animal is sacrificed in connection with the naming. The ritual is more elaborate when the newborn is a boy. In cases where the child is taught to read, the first book will be the Kor'an. It is also often the *only* textbook. Portions of the Kor'an are learned by heart and can be recited word for word. That is the purpose of the Kor'anic schools.

Boys and girls may play together until they reach puberty.

After that they are segregated. The girl's dress will be according to Muslim rules that still vary from country to country and culture to culture.

When the boys reach the age of seven circumcision takes place. Also here there are variations in various cultures and Muslim traditions. Circumcision, though practised widely among Muslims, is not mandatory from a religious standpoint. It is, however, a ritual or custom followed among Muslims worldwide. New converts to Islam are not required to be circumcised, but many will follow the custom. In connection with the circumcision, a celebration takes place with the sacrifice of a sheep or other animal. Circumcision has two meanings for the boy. From a spiritual standpoint, at the age of seven he is deemed to have sufficient knowledge of the Kor'an and Islamic teaching to know the difference between right and wrong. Biologically, circumcision gives the boy the right to be an active member of the Muslim community and, together with the men, take part in the daily prayers, the fast, and the other pillars of Islam.

The controversial issue of the repugnant practice of female circumcision is also not required by Islamic law and has no religious sanction. It is a cultural practice in parts of Africa. It is probably something inherited from people with a background of traditional religions. With other non-Islamic cultural practices it has been brought into Islam. It helps to form what is called Folk-Islam. In general Muslim leaders do not approve of it.

Marriage

Marriages are usually arranged affairs in Muslim society, even among Muslims who have settled in Christian countries. As a rule the bridegroom's family takes the initiative.

Often it is within the extended family that the search for a suitable partner takes place. Marriages between cousins are common. During the times of 'engagements' the couples have no right to be alone together.

The marriage is a kind of contract and in many cases a 'dowry' is paid to the bride's family. It is recommended that even in arranged marriages the wishes of the bride are taken into consideration. However, that is not always the case. The prearranged *forced* marriages we hear about too often among Muslims who live among us are serious problems for young Muslim girls who grow up in a Western culture.

Girls can be married when they are only 12 years old. It is of vital importance that the bride enters the marriage as a virgin. The loss of virginity can be a very serious matter. In extreme cases, the relatives of the bride, in order to save the honour of the family, have been known to kill a girl who has lost her virginity. The 'honorary murders' of girls who have had sexual relations with Western (Christian) males are defended by *Shar'iah* law.

The wedding ceremony as a rule is not conducted in the mosque. It takes place in a hall rented and equipped for the purpose. Sometimes the home is the setting for the celebrations, and the festivities are often costly affairs conducted according to local customs.

Death

The face of the dying person is turned towards Mecca while the *Shahada* is repeatedly either said by the dying person or whispered into his or her ear. This is in preparation for meeting Izrail, 'the angel of death'. Even after the Muslim has passed away, relatives and friends will continue whispering the *Shahada*, sometimes for up to seven hours. Persons of the same sex will wash the dead person and there will also be a ritual cleansing. The funeral, whenever possible, will take place before sunset on the day of death. Generally no coffin is used. The body is shrouded in a winding cloth, and carried on the shoulders of men to the grave. Women do not normally take part in the funeral procession. In the grave the body is placed so the face is turned towards Mecca. The grave of a Muslim should not be disturbed. It is expected that it will remain untouched until the day of judgement.

The role of women in Islam

The Muslim community represents a patriarchy. This means that the social organisation and domestic life are characterised by the domination of men. This, of course, has a decisive influence on the family life and the role of women. The Kor'an has more verses on the role, duties, rights and social status of women in the Muslim society than on any other subject. The Kor'an and the prophetic traditions, in some cases, do reveal a reasonable equal-rights attitude between the sexes. *Sura* 49, 13 points out that all people stem from one man and one woman. The noblest among them is the most righteous. And in the Hadith Muhammad has expressed that:

'All people are equal, as equal as the teeth of a comb. An Arab is no better than a non-Arab, nor is a white person better than a black person, nor is the male superior to the female. The only people who enjoy preference with God are the devout.' So, in theory, the issue of equal status between the sexes is clear, and is established in some of the texts.

Equality between men and women, however, does not mean that they are identical. The woman has a distinct and separate identity from the man, mainly due to psychological, physical and biological characteristics. In this way men and women complement each other, and for that reason Allah created them as a team. It is a fact that in Islam the man is the leader of the home and the ruler of the woman. There is no doubt that in Muslim society the woman has an inferior position.

It is expected that the Muslim wife will give priority to children, home and family. The *Shar'iah* law limits to a great extent her role, activities and responsibilities in society. It must be admitted that Muhammad improved the lives of women compared with their lot in Mecca at the Times of Ignorance before he appeared on the scene.

Islam gives women an interesting status with a combination of limited freedom but great security. Muhammad limited, to a great degree, the unworthy and rough treatment they were exposed to at the hands of men. He forbade the murder of newborn unwanted girls. The exploitation of maids and slave women in Mecca was also forbidden. At the same time, however, he limited by law women's rights and privileges, their personal freedom and development. It could be maintained that Muhammad set both the floor and ceiling for the position of women in Muslim societies.

The dress of Muslim women

The Muslim lifestyle is particularly obvious, compared with the Western, in the way the women are dressed. Some are dressed in costumes that would fit well into the Mecca of the seventh century, the time of Muhammad. These traditional dress rules for women have to be followed when a girl reaches the age of puberty. When a Muslim woman is in a place where she will meet men who are not her relatives, she has to have her whole body covered.

The rules for covering the face vary from culture to culture. Some Islamic areas demand that the face is covered in such a way that recognition is impossible. Some women see the world through a veil somewhat like a sieve. Others cover all except the eyes. Then there are some who cover only the hair.

The Kor'an recommended that the wives of Muhammad wore the veil, but it was commonly used only 150 years after the death of the prophet. None of the many *Shar'iah* law schools orders the wearing of the veil, although most recommend it. While modesty in dress is a religious decree, the wearing of the veil is a cultural matter. There are many Muslim women who wear European dress while they are in the West, though Muslim communities do not generally accept this. Within the walls of the home Muslim women can dress as they please as long as only the near family is present.

Generally speaking, Muslim women follow the strict dress codes because the *Shar'iah*, culture or family dictates them. No doubt the women's dress in Islam renders a certain protection against unwanted passes. Some are obedient to the codes because the male family members demand it.

Perhaps the whole philosophy behind the Muslim restrictions on what can be seen of the woman's beauty and form, on her style of clothing, her social life, and the people she is allowed to mix with, is to be found in the Islamic understanding of temptation. In Christianity we are taught not only to avoid temptation and to stand against it, we are also encouraged to pray for power to resist. In the Lord's Prayer we say: 'Lead us not into temptation.'

In the Islamic understanding the male is weak and easily

tempted to fall, and the female is a temptation. In the Kor'an man is admonished to lower his gaze when he is in the company of, or meets, a woman. In his fight against sexual temptation, the man is fortified as Islam covers or even removes what could be tempting. Women are covered; socialising with them is forbidden; places of entertainment are closed; and prostitutes are executed. A legalistic religion has helped its adherents not to break the rules. At least *assistance* to keep the letter of the law has been supplied!

The Muslim marriage

One of the more problematic areas for the Muslim woman is the fact that her husband is allowed to have four wives in addition to concubines. Permission for polygamy is found in Sura 4:3:

'If ye fear that ye shall not be able to deal justly with the orphans, marry women of your choice, two or three, or four; but if ye fear that ye shall not be able to deal justly (with them), then only one, or that which your right hand possesses. That will be more suitable, to prevent you from doing injustice.'

There were more reasons for allowing men to have four wives simultaneously. One was the war against Mecca. Muhammad and his followers fought wars at the dawn of Islam. These naturally left many widows and orphans, and the most convenient way to solve the problem was to marry the widow and the unmarried daughters and thereby make them members of the harem. Polygamy was practised on the Arabian Peninsula before Muhammad began his preaching. Many Muslims defend the custom, claiming that polygamy is to be preferred to secret unfaithfulness, prostitution or having mistresses. Muslims are keen to point out these abuses among 'Christian' men.

A Muslim woman enjoys the rights and privileges that befit her nature. At least this is the way the many restrictions are interpreted. Her father, uncle, brother, husband and son try to compensate for the limitations they put on her life by granting her security and diminished responsibility. In cultures where the main purpose of marriage is to produce children and secure offspring, polygamy is also defended with the argument that the childless, barren or chronically sick wife is not pushed out of the marriage but remains and keeps the status that marriage brings.

Another argument used to defend polygamy is that more girls than boys are born into the world. That is not always the case. However, women spend more years in marriage. They are married at an earlier age than men, they live longer, and in many societies men are, by their work, often exposed to fatal accidents. Though polygamy is, as mentioned, allowed in Islam, few marriages are, in fact, polygamous. There would not be sufficient women to be co-wives even if only one in twenty Muslim men were to practise polygamy.

Divorce, birth control and inheritance

Allah allows divorce. However, Muhammad regarded it is as 'the most hateful of lawful things'. A man can repudiate his wife simply by saying: 'I divorce you!' He can do that twice and still take her back. The third time he says the word it is irreversible. He can then only take her back if, in the meantime, she has been married to another man and has been widowed or her new marriage has been dissolved. The family is expected to do all they can to save the marriage and the couple should be under the same roof for three months. During this time they are not allowed to have sexual intercourse. This period of waiting is not only to get the married couple reconciled; it is to find out if the wife is pregnant.

According to Muslim rules and customs the father always has custody of the children. They can stay with the mother until they reach the age of seven years. Then the father will take over. Where the mother is a non-Muslim, after a divorce the father always gets custody of the children. They must be brought up in the Islamic faith.

It is hard for a Muslim wife to get a divorce. It can be obtained in a peaceful way by a mutual agreement between the partners. It can also be a legal decision where the wife has to give very valid reasons for her wishes to be divorced. Impotence, mental illness and apostasy from Islam are counted as sound reasons.

A Muslim man has the right to marry a Christian or Jewish woman, as each belongs to an Abrahamic religion. The non-Muslim wife is allowed to practise her religion in private. In reality that is not always the case. When Muslims report that many Westerners have converted to Islam, a further examination of the statistics will reveal that the majority of the converts are women married to Muslim men. In these cross-religion marriages the woman can be exposed to coercion to leave her Christian faith. A Muslim woman cannot marry a Christian man.

Birth control by artificial means is disapproved of in Islam. Such practices, it is claimed, will not only destabilise the family; they will also hinder the growth and spread of Islam. The Muslim man wants as many children as possible. Abortion is allowed only in extreme cases and should take place within the first four months of the pregnancy.

Other rules and laws in Islam regarding the role of women state that in questions of inheritance the daughters receive only half the amount that the sons will get. In court cases two women are required to make up the testimony witness of one man. In social relationships Muslim women can meet and entertain only women or men who are closely related. As already mentioned, a woman can take part in the pilgrimage to Mecca, the high point in Islam's spiritual life, only when her husband or a close male relative accompanies her. When a woman wants to attend the daily prayers in the mosque (and a very small percentage of them do so regularly), she has to worship separately and unseen by the male worshippers.

To all this must be added that in Muhammad's country of birth a woman has no right to drive a car and no right to go and eat in a restaurant alone. At the bank she has to use her own entrance and is served at a counter where only women serve women. A Muslim girl's opportunity to receive an education is very limited; therefore illiteracy among Muslim women is very high.

Muslims will claim that in Islam the women have equal status with men, but it is very obvious that this is only in theory. Muslim women have a second-class status. They are definitely placed on a much lower level. Nevertheless, it must be said that the status of women varies greatly from one Muslim country to another. In rare cases women have risen to high positions both in politics and business in some Muslim countries.

chapter 8

Diet, art, and Islamic Sects

Islam's strict dietary programme serves two purposes. First it is cultic in that compliance with the rules for what you eat, how you eat and with whom you eat is also a condition for entering paradise. Secondly, the same rules are part of a health programme that will promote well-being and avert disease.

Food and drink should not be taken for granted. These gifts come from Allah and should be accepted with gratitude and used reasonably for the benefit of the Muslim's health. All food should be nourishing, even tasty. The purpose of food is not only to bring good physical health, but to strengthen moral and spiritual health.

The Kor'anic dietary plan for animal consumption

✳ Animals (*Sura* 16:5-8)

The list of animals that are fit for human consumption generally follows the diet outlined in the Old Testament's Book of Leviticus. There are some important exceptions.

Allowed: (*Sura* 5:5) The Kor'an has very specific and detailed rules for animals. Generally, domestic animals are allowed for consumption, though some animals killed in hunting are accepted as food – animals that chew the cud such as the cow, buffalo, deer, antelope, sheep, goat, etc.

Included are also animals with clean eating habits (camel, rabbit).

Forbidden: Carnivorous animals; beasts of burden (horse, donkey, mule, but not the camel).

A *'Bismillah'*, a consecration to Allah, must be said before slaughter. In Western abattoirs that export meat to Muslim countries, an Imam is paid for this service.

* **Plants (*Sura* 20:53, 54)**

Allowed: Fruits, grains, oil-seed crops, herbs and similar plants.

Forbidden: Intoxicants, poisonous plants, and others which cause harm to the body. Tobacco is forbidden in Islam. However, in general, this prohibition is not enforced.

* **Sea Food (*Sura* 16:14)**

Allowed: All seafood including the blood.

Forbidden: Seafood which died on its own.

No Bismillah needed.

* **Insects**

Allowed: Locusts and grasshoppers.

* **Intoxicating drinks (*Sura* 5:92)** All forms of alcohol are strictly forbidden, though allowed as medicine.

* **Summary:**

Forbidden in Islam:
 a. Pork and blood.
 b. Alcohol, tobacco and drugs.
 c. Animals not slaughtered in accordance with Islamic rituals.

d. Vessels used for food and certain foods can also be declared unfit for human consumption. In life-threatening situations prohibited food may be eaten.

Muslim dietary rules and table manners are not limited to food. Some Islamic traditions, specially the *Shi'ites*, have additional rules that make it clear that persons and things can also be unclean. People can be defiled by not having the 'right' religion. This applies not only to Hindus, Christians and Jews, but even Muslims from traditions other than the *Shi'ites*. Pots and pans, plates and cutlery are also defiled when they have previously been in contact with unclean food or food that has not been blessed by a *Bismillah*. A defiled person can make eating utensils unclean.

In connection with the dietary laws and regulations, Islam is also proving itself as a religion with interesting dispensations. Under especially trying conditions, a Muslim is exempted from following the rules. Unclean food such as pork is allowed for consumption in circumstances where the person is threatened with starvation. There are four conditions for breaking the strict rules. No clean food should be available; the hunger should have lasted for at least twelve hours, the person should just eat sufficient to survive the next twelve hours and it is forbidden to say that the unclean food is tasty.

Cultic Health Principles

The positive effect of a strict observance of Islamic health laws on the faithful Muslim is noteworthy. Obedience to these rules according to the Kor'an and the Hadith is an important part of faith, even a condition for entering paradise.

These laws for health and hygiene include food, as we have seen, with a detailed list of unclean animals, prohibitions against alcohol and drugs, even tobacco (although the rules there are somewhat slack). Also included in the cultic health rules is a yearly period of fasting for 28 days, which, if adhered to, can be of importance for physical well-being.

The five-times-daily prayers are, to some extent, also physical exercises in which the worshipper, in the course of the five periods, sits down, stands up, kneels and prostrates on the ground many times. The forehead of a Muslim who is strictly following the prayer rules will daily touch the ground 34 times. In connection with prayers there are ablutions. This means that the face, hands and feet are generally washed five times daily, and the whole body at least once. Even the place where the Muslim prays should be clean.

A scrupulously careful Muslim obeying all the Islamic dietary and health regulations will have the makings of a healthy life. Christians with advanced modern medical science and research will readily endorse these principles. The Bible, however, does not impose such strict rules on the Christian's lifestyle, although there are suggestions for the right food and temperance. The purpose of these instructions is to promote physical health and hygiene. They are not conditions of salvation.

Other areas of the Muslim lifestyle

The Islamic calendar began on 15 July 622 when Muhammad fled from Mecca to Medina. While we are in the twenty-first century, the Muslims are in the fifteenth century. The Islamic year is based on the moon and has 12 months, alternately 29 and 30 days long. This makes the Islamic year about 10 days shorter than the Christian year, which follows the Gregorian calendar. The result is that the gap in recording time between the two calendars is constantly widening.

This shorter calendar is an inconvenience for Muslims who live in Northern latitudes. As mentioned, during Ramadan (month of fast) Muslims can eat only between sunset and sunrise. In the course of about 18 years the fast will move from summer to winter or winter to summer. This is not a big problem for the majority of Muslims living near the equator. For the few Muslim emigrants living beyond the Arctic Circle, however, a Ramadan falling in the winter will allow them to eat normally as there is only night in the winter months. Eighteen years later, with a summer Ramadan, there will be no permission to eat for four weeks! The problem is solved by following Mecca time.

Islam puts limitations on the use of art. On a visit to a mosque one quickly discovers that visual expressions of art are absent. There are no pictures, sculptures, statues or other works of art. Absent, also, in the service itself are songs and music. The religious sentiments and emotions of Muslims can find expression only in calligraphy and architecture. And in these two areas Islamic people have contributed greatly to the world of visual arts. Calligraphy in the Arabic language, applied in connection with the writing of the Kor'an, is internationally appreciated and valued.

The Muslim believes that the Kor'an, word for word, came directly from Allah to Muhammad, therefore writing the words is a sacred task that demands extreme care. The task of writing is itself regarded as a kind of worship, with an aura of holy dedication connected to it. The copyists have shown imagination and great inventiveness in writing the twenty-eight letters of the Arabic alphabet. They have indeed made their alphabet one of the most beautiful in the world.

The same dedication is demonstrated in architecture. When building mosques Muslims also have an outlet for their religious devotion. For this reason mosques are generally beautiful and attractive buildings where the imagination of the architect, controlled by Islamic religious concepts, has an opportunity to express religious feeling. In Muslim villages, even in poor areas, the mosque is generally outstanding and is the building of greatest value. The same, of course, goes for Christian churches. These factors must be valued as positive expressions of the dedication of Muslims.

Regarding businesses and banks, the Kor'an forbids any form of income based on interest. In Islamic concepts *Riba*, the Arabic word for it, has a tendency to increase the wealth of the rich and bring the poor into greater debt. In the modern business world, with which Muslims are involved, such principles for banking and financial undertakings are hard to put into practice, though they were no doubt adequate for the business transactions in the city and Bedouin society a thousand years ago. The prohibition is often ignored. The *riba* is then classified as commission, a necessary expense in connection with the administration of the loan.

In Islamic societies there is no priesthood in the sense that we have in Christian churches. In the mosque, however, there is a person who leads out in the five daily prayer sessions. The prayer leader is called *sheik, mullah* or *imam*, according to which Islamic tradition he serves. It is an unpaid, honorary task that as a rule falls on a male person in the congregation, of good reputation, being the right age, and with adequate knowledge of Islam and efficiency in the Arabic language. There is no ordination in Islam. All are 'priests' in the sense that all Muslims can lead out in the rituals connected with religion. The salaried religious experts in Islam such as judges, legal experts or teachers in theology are also experts in *Shar'iah* law.

Reasons for variations in Muslim patterns of life

The few examples mentioned above are the areas where the Muslim lifestyle is visibly different from the lifestyles of Europeans. For this reason the selected points mentioned are very general. All Muslims whom you meet do not all have the same lifestyles or the same religious convictions. They have various cultural backgrounds. Their individual personalities also play important roles in their conduct.

The attitudes some Muslims have to their beliefs and rituals vary greatly from those of the orthodox fundamentalists who take the words of the Kor'an and the Shar'iah literally. They are the most well known. On the other hand, there are many, perhaps a majority of Muslims, with a liberal attitude to life and religion, who will generally pay only superficial attention to a few of the most fundamental of the Muslim beliefs and rituals.

The Muslims in Western lands have their roots in countries that stretch from Morocco to Indonesia, from Kazakstan to Somalia. Their great dissimilarities in cultural backgrounds will, of course, be shaping their lifestyles, even in religious matters.

Islamic sects

When Muslims talk about Christianity, they look on all Christians as belonging to one massive, unified and homogeneous group. They perceive no difference among Anglicans, Presbyterians, Roman Catholics, Baptists, Adventists and Pentecostals. A Christian is a Christian. A Muslim does not discern that there are differences in doctrinal teachings. All this in spite of the fact that there are more than 30,000 traditions and sects.

In the same way, Christians are often inclined to look at Muslims as a big, monolithic, uniform mass all adhering to the same religion. To us *they* seem a homogeneous group of people with the same beliefs, customs and habits, but, like Christianity, Islam consists of many different traditions or sects. The two most important are the *Sunni* and *Shi'ite* traditions. The main difference between these two traditions is that where the Sunnis believe that the final authority is vested in the accepted scriptural material, the Shi'as are concerned with the prophetic succession. They feel that the authority is in the leader of the Muslim world community. And he should come from the family of the prophet Muhammad. These two main groups are again divided into perhaps more than *500* religious traditions. We will mention a few of the most important ones such as the *Wahabites, Ahmadiyas, Alawites, Zaidites, Imanites,* and *Ismalites*. These are also divided into groups on the basis of national, linguistic and tribal connections.

All are in agreement on the principal points in Islam, the belief in Allah, the Kor'an, and Muhammad as the prophet of Allah. Most Islamic sects are able to meet in Mecca in connection with the pilgrimage events, although the members of some sects are denied access to the holy city.

Divisions arise generally on questions of lifestyle and leadership. In many cases there are physical fights to the death between different groups.

Folk Islam

The Muslims can also be divided into orthodox and syncretistic Muslims. Truly orthodox believing Muslims know the demands of the *Shar'iah* law and all the rules in Islam. They live in areas where the government and laws are generally based on Islamic principles. For that reason, society and their environment as a whole are geared so that their lifestyle is determined and they have few other choices.

These, the most orthodox Muslims, are usually Arabs living reasonably close to Mecca, where Islam has been the only religion for generations. Other religions have been suppressed or in other ways eliminated.

As Islam spread out from the Arabian Peninsula 1,400 years ago to non-Arab nations, the Muslims had some success among people who had backgrounds in either Hinduism or African traditional religions.

The requirement for being a Muslim was often just a recital of the *Shahada* in Arabic. This easily-fulfilled condition produced many who were Muslim in name only. Important aspects of the old religion that for centuries had given meaning to life remained or were incorporated into Islam in one way or another. The matter of what happens after death, where the Asians believed in incarnation and the Africans in ancestor worship, became a real test for the new believers and the Muslims. The new syncretistic religion is called Folk-Islam.

It is suggested that the great majority of Muslims worldwide are practising a Folk-Islamic religion in which the orthodox Islamic belief is mixed up with beliefs and superstitions from other religions. One result of this Folk-Islamic religion has been that both the lifestyle and content of Islam are very superficial.

Reluctantly, it seems today, Muslim leaders expect a Muslim living outside areas where *Shar'iah* law has its influence to be faithful in only three main points of faith. He or she must believe in Allah, the Kor'an as his revealed will, and Muhammad as the last prophet. The observance of the various rituals and the Muslim lifestyle is naturally desired but not enforced. *Imams* are prepared to accept conduct that would entail strict punishment in areas where *Shar'iah* law holds sway.

Sufism - the Mysticism in Islam

In spite of, or perhaps as a result of, the strict religious rules of Islam, a kind of mysticism called *Sufism* emerged early in the history of the religion. This mysticism served to some extent as a safety valve for believers who felt a need to escape from the rigorous and legalistic demands Islam laid on them. *Sufi* originates from the Arabic word for wool, and was a term applied to the mystics because they lived under primitive conditions as hermits and wore coarse woollen clothes. The *Sufis* were the kinds of people who reacted against the Muslim rulers and clergy who lived in luxury. These mystics renounced the world and sought a spiritual union with Allah.

Sufis stressed the inward spiritual experience with the desire to be rid of self and be part of the divine.

Sufis have throughout the history of Islam been exposed to persecution from the religious establishment. This in spite of the fact that they never aspired to political power, or even control of Islam. *Sufism* is a popular movement operating in the whole Muslim world across all traditions and sects.

Contrary to the general negative attitudes in Islam to most forms of art, the *Sufis* introduced song, music, dance and poetry as a component of their religious services. By offering the worshippers an expected direct access to Allah, *Sufism* in its own way, contributed to weakening the influence of the Kor'an, the *Hadith* and the *Shar'iah* law. In some cases the result was a moral laxness and superficial obedience to the Islamic rules and regulations.

chapter 9

Islam in the twenty-first century

Only a few years after the death of Muhammad, Islam began its extensive conquests in North Africa and Southern Europe. As a result a relationship with tensions of both religious and political character began between Muslims and Christians. This situation, with various kinds of conflicts, has existed ever since. It has often provided the excuse for persecution and open bloody warfare, not to mention ethnic cleansings.

Both Muslims and Christians are guilty of such abuse. One cause for the tensions in the religious arena is that both Christianity and Islam are world religions. Christians and Muslims alike believe that only they have the correct understanding of all questions that have to do with life now and in the hereafter, as well as the way to salvation, and that this belief must be proclaimed to all inhabitants of the world. Adherents of other religions must be persuaded to change. When this does not happen, in far too many cases force is used. They are both equally guilty.

The Mediterranean Sea

Wars in the past were fought not only to win new converts. There were also strong political motives. Once, the Mediterranean Sea separated the Christians and Muslims.

Islamic people ruled the southern and eastern shores, while Roman Catholic and Greek Orthodox churches controlled the northern coastline.

On these coastlines the prominent cultures, African, Asiatic and European, met. The Eastern Mediterranean was the cradle of the three monotheistic religions: Judaism, Christianity and Islam. Economically and politically the jurisdiction also had enormous value. For centuries ships on this water brought raw materials, spices, cotton and other goods to Europe. Here they were manufactured and returned and sold with great profit. Later, oil became an extremely important element in the power game.

At the Mediterranean, East and West, North and South met. The Catholic and Orthodox Christians on the northern side had great influence on the southern countries. They were outraged and humiliated when the countries where the history of the Bible had its origin were, one after the other, conquered by Muslims. Even Palestine, where Jesus Christ lived and worked, became a Muslim-dominated country. The same went for North Africa, where one of the greatest Christian theologians had his calling. Augustine of Hippo wasarchbishop in what today is Algeria. Only 300 years after his death the country was conquered by Muslim soldiers who forced the Berbers to accept Islam – the same armies that in AD732 conquered what is now Spain, Portugal, Southern France and Sicily. These areas, however, were later recaptured. But Northern Africa remained under Islamic rule.

The Ottoman Empire – the Colonial Era

Constantinople became the capital of the Byzantine Empire in AD395. During the Fourth Crusade in 1204 the town was besieged, conquered and destroyed by the crusaders. This was one of the many atrocities of the crusades. In 1453 the Muslim Turks, the Ottomans, conquered the city and made it the capital of the Ottoman Empire. The city was renamed Istanbul, and from this capital for more than 400 years the Ottomans ruled over Syria, Jordan, Palestine, Saudi Arabia, Yemen and the islands in the Aegean Sea.

Until World War I it was a Turk with the title of caliph who heavy-handedly ruled a great proportion of the Muslims in the world. The Ottoman Empire had all the characteristics of a colonial power. It was, however, not regarded as such by the Muslims, owing to the fact that it was a caliphate, and therefore in Islamic understanding the ideal form of government.

During the regime of the caliph, Islam was taken to and accepted by many in the Balkans. In both the sixteenth and seventeenth centuries Turkish (Ottoman) armies marched on Vienna. The Polish army, plus a severe winter with snow and ice, stopped them. Islam, however, kept its hold on parts of the Balkans. The sultan combined his caliphate 'sacred' position, where he was the spiritual leader of Muslims, with political power. The caliphate reached its zenith around 1550. Until the middle of the nineteenth century, on the world scene Islam was a power to be reckoned with.

There were, however, some humiliating setbacks for the Muslims. During the period of the crusades (1096-1270) European potentates were inspired by the noble motive of freeing the Holy Land from Islamic rule. Muslims still talk about the atrocities these European princes committed against them.

The crusaders professed a noble Christian aim. Ostensibly, it was to free the land of Christ from the infidels, but the crusades might also conceivably have had something to do with impoverished princes seeking precious treasures in exotic lands.

Half a millennium later the colonial era began in earnest. The Muslim area under the rule of the caliph in Istanbul ended up under the rule of the big colonial powers. Great Britain, France, Italy, Spain and the Netherlands shared the Muslim countries among themselves. Those areas that did not come directly under the control of these European powers were in one way or another dependent on them. It must be mentioned that all the colonial powers were considered 'Christian' nations.

At the end of the nineteenth century the Turkish Empire was so weakened that the Sultan was nicknamed the 'Sick Man of Europe'. The Islamic nations after their time under the caliphate and later colonial experience had very little influence even on local conditions. In world politics they were generally excluded; not rated highly in the political arena. And should Muslim leaders show ambition in the direction of more self-government, expansion of territories or even complete independence, the colonial masters would make sure that such attempts were nipped in the bud. Centuries-long humiliations such as the crusades, colonial rule and dependence on the West still affect in a negative way the attitudes of Muslims to Western countries.

The Years after the Second World War

The Second World War weakened the colonial powers in spite of the fact that most of them were on the winning side. World opinion indicated that the time for granting independence to the colonies had come. Muslim countries in general received their sovereignty by 1950. At the same time, new discoveries of oil on the Arabian Peninsula and the resulting oil production gave not only a great economic boom for the prophet Muhammad's native country, but the new situation, bringing financial independence, gave Muslims much-needed self-confidence. 'Allah has blessed us with a powerful tool, the oil!' they said.

But the processes connected with the negotiations and fight for independence did not take place without some bitterness. The procedure involved birth pains and bloodshed. The new Islamic nations (kingdoms or republic-type governments) had to rediscover their own identities, learn how to rule independently, find their places in the international community, and build up political systems and structure in their own societies. Legal systems had to be established. A few introduced the *Shar'iah* law. All these processes resulting from independence were painful and complicated and caused many internal and external struggles.

The awakening of the Islamic people after more than 200 years of hibernation caused a revival that was expressed in a variety of ways.

Politically this renascence gave new life to Arabic (Islamic) nationalism, and the foremost promoter in this area was President Gamel Abdel Nasser of Egypt. He was an army officer, strongly opposed to Western influences on the Arabs, who introduced 'Arab Socialism'. That resulted in a new party, the Arab Socialist Union, with a programme appealing to Arab nationalism. Arab self-confidence was, no doubt, strongly influenced by Islam, but even non-Arab Muslims were inspired by this movement.

Economically it gave the Arabs an international political striking power, in the shape not only of control of oil production but of oil prices. Religiously the new situation inspired fervent activity. Millions were killed in the internal and external conflicts.

Mention should be made briefly of the civil war in Lebanon, the war between Iraq and Iran and Iraq's attack on Kuwait.

Extreme Muslims in Sudan, Egypt, Nigeria, Indonesia, the Philippines and Pakistan have persecuted and killed Christians.

Islamic fanatics in Algeria, Pakistan and Egypt are attacking other Muslims, who they claim do not live up to the claims of the *Shar'iah*.

China, India, Russia and the USA are now beginning to be attacked on their own soil, and innocent Western tourists are killed and kidnapped as part of Muslims' religious and political goals.

The two chief reasons for dissatisfaction

Today more than ever the word *jihad* (holy war) against the *kufr* (infidels) is on the lips of millions of young Muslims all over the world.

There are several motivations for the fiendish attitudes against all that is non-Islamic, especially in the West. No doubt there is a degree of dissatisfaction with the lack of development and with the poverty in most Islamic countries in the world, compared with the West and some of the countries in the Pacific basin.

In this connection it will be in place to quote one of the most powerful leaders in the Muslim world on this delicate subject:

'The president of Pakistan, General Pevaiz Musharraf, encourages the Muslim countries to create a multibillion fund to promote science and technology. The reason is that Muslim nations in these areas are far behind the rest of the world. Muslims are the poorest, least privileged, most unhealthy and most ignorant people in the world. While

Muslim countries have a quarter of the world's population and 70 per cent of all energy resources, their national product is only one fifth of what Japan produces. And while Japan has more than 1,000 universities, Muslim countries have only 420. There is a call for a holy war against poverty.'
(Translated from Denmark's Radio-Sl43, 17 February 2002.)

This revealing and very direct observation is made by one of the most prominent Islamic leaders. These sentiments were not expressed by a Christian. General Musharraf is president of an Islamic nation with more than 140 million people. No doubt, the facts expressed in the quotation will give rise to feelings of shame and inferiority among many Muslims. They will naturally draw comparisons with the standard of living, technology and social benefits they watch people in the West enjoying. The differences between the two worlds are obvious for Muslims who either visit or live in the West. Those who do not have that opportunity will, through television, films and other media, draw their own conclusions.

It does not require much imagination to visualise the reactions. Muslims are brought up in centuries of tradition where pride and honour are given great importance and where losing face is humiliating. In that humiliation they turn against developed nations, especially Christian countries.

Calling a *jihad* (holy war) is not only a religious move. It is also a political one. Proud Muslims watch the very tense situation, including open conflict between Jews and Arabs in Israel, which they call Palestine. They know that Israel's survival to a great extent is dependent on the heavy support it receives from the USA and also some Western European countries. They have experienced how a 'Christian' nation has bombarded Libya, Iraq, Somalia,

Afghanistan and Iraq. Add to this the bitter pill they have had to swallow that American (Christian?) soldiers are stationed in Saudi Arabia, walking the land where the prophet Muhammad had his call and ministry.

To all these humiliations they have to add the indignity of knowing that many of their own Muslim nations are run by corrupt governments led by greedy politicians and public servants. These are perceived as not only exploiting their positions to their own benefit but paying only lip-service to Islam, while acting as stooges for those who are filling their pockets with dollars.

The Call to Jihad

'We have to start a holy war. This is the only solution to our plight.' The reaction of the radical Muslim to all these humiliations is *jihad*. The Arabic word has its root in a word which means spiritual strife. This strife can be for a worthy cause, or channelled through military campaigns the purpose of which is spreading or defending Islam.

The concept of *jihad* comes from a fundamental principle in the universal character of Islam. It is understood that Islam is not only a religion but also a political system. It is the aim that the whole world shall join the religion of Islam, and the belief is that the 'secular', political power can assist in making that a reality. In other words, when people will not join by free will through persuasion, the rabid Muslim will go to the extreme and force conversion by military might.

The principle of world domination where religion and government are joined together is, however, combined with another principle in Islam. There is toleration for people belonging to the 'people of the book' (Abrahamic religions with the holy books) – Jews and Christians. For these monotheists the holy war will cease the moment they recognise and are subject to the Islamic authorities and pay a certain tax levied on non-Muslims. In a more modern understanding it is generally accepted that the spread of Islam is based on persuasion and other means.

The humiliating realities such as poverty and backwardness, combined with political and military defeats, are able to awaken a militant attitude that can easily be channelled into a call to *jihad*. Nationalism, economic control and religious awakening in the last 50 years have not been able to bring about appreciable improvements in conditions for Muslims in their home countries. For that reason people like Osama bin Laden decided to turn against the enemy with a holy war. And they can use the Kor'an and the traditions to defend this *jihad*. It depends on which texts or passages they put into focus and emphasise and which they choose to ignore. Both the Kor'an and the *Hadiths* have texts that deal with and promote peace and good treatment of non-Muslims. There are, however, also passages from the same books that call for war against those who oppose Islam.

In *Surat* 9:5-6 we read:

'But when the forbidden months are past, then fight and slay the pagans wherever ye find them, and seize them, beleaguer them, and lie in wait for them in every stratagem [of war]; but if they repent, and establish regular prayers and pay Zakat, open the way for them: For Allah is Oft-forgiving, Most Merciful.'

This Kor'anic text, among so many others with the same negative message, can easily be interpreted as pointing to Christians who believe in a Trinity. As a matter of fact, the Kor'an states directly that unbelievers are those who say that 'Allah is Christ', the son of Mary. In *Surah* 5:7 we read:

'They disbelieved indeed those that say that Allah is Christ the son of Mary: "Who then hath the least power against Allah, if His will were to destroy Christ the son of Mary, his mother and all – every one that is on the earth?"'
Surah 5:72-73:

'Certainly they disbelieve who say: "Allah is the Christ the son of Mary." But said Christ: "O Children of Israel! Worship Allah, my Lord and your Lord." Whoever joins other gods with Allah, Allah will forbid him the Garden and the Fire will be his abode. There will for the wrongdoers be no one to help.

'They disbelieve who say: Allah is one of three (in a Trinity:) for there is no god except one God. If they desist not from their word (of blasphemy), verily grievous chastisement will befall the disbelievers, among them.'

The holy war, the *jihad*, is not one of the Five Pillars in Islam. The call for this kind of war should be only in cases of extreme emergency, when the Muslim world is attacked or the existence of Islam as a religion is threatened. No doubt the most extreme Muslims deemed that this was the case when the 11 September events were planned, justified by a *fatwa* and executed. The Kor'an and the *Hadith* were used, not only to defend the decision for the cruel attacks; the holy writings in Islam were also applied to get volunteers for these suicide attacks for what Muslims called actions of martyrs.

The 'Abode of War', the 'Abode of Islam'

In the Muslim understanding of life the world is divided into two distinct areas: the abode of war *(Dar al-Harb)* and the abode of Islam *(Dar al-Islam)*. The abode of war is the territories where Islam is not in charge or control, in other words where the *Shar'iah* law is not in force; for instance,

Christian Europe, Hindu Nepal – even India, countries belonging to the 'war area'. In contrast, Allah's will, as expressed in the *Shar'iah*, is the authority in the abode of Islam *(Dar al-Islam)* where Muslims live. It is significant that the designation 'abode of war' is applied to areas where, among others, Christians live.

The successors of Muhammad received the title caliph. The caliph is both the religious and the secular ruler of the Islamic world. He is regarded as the successor of Muhammad and as such he has the same position and office as the prophet. The difference is that the direct call to prophethood applies only to Muhammad, who was the last prophet.

Thus the office of the caliphate is a spiritual office and not merely secular. This adds mystical aspects to the leader of a secular government. Perhaps the best, but not perfect, comparison would be the office of the Pope in the Roman Catholic Church. In addition to being called the 'Vicar of God on Earth' he is also the secular head of the Vatican State. As such he receives ambassadors from various secular governments. Kemal Ataturk abolished the 'Turkish' caliphate in 1924.

Today, however, there is a call to re-establish the caliphate. The idea is to join the more than 50 nations with majority Muslim populations together under one caliph. Should this scheme of a *Dar al-Islam* ever be a reality it would create a religious/secular nation comprising up to one billion people. It would stretch over four continents, controlling most of the oil reserves of the world. The government and inhabitants would live under the strict *Shar'iah* law. One of the tasks of this caliphate would then be to bring the rule of Allah and the *Shar'iah* into the 'abode of war' *(Dar al-Harb)*.

This plan is far from being a reality. The Muslim world is divided into more than 50 countries, with various styles of government ranging from democratic republics, dictatorships and sultanates to kingdoms. And these countries have various degrees of conformity to Islam. They often wage war on one another, probably because Arab nationalism – introduced by Nasser – is stronger in the mind of the ordinary Muslim than the caliphate concept. This concept, however, is really more in accordance with the Islamic world-view. The caliphate is far from being a thing of the near future. Although texts and passages from the Kor'an can be interpreted to defend a holy war to gather Muslims into a worldwide brotherhood of nations, it must be stated that Islam has generally spread to neighbouring nations by peaceful means.

However, deep in Islamic self-understanding, the relationship to Christians was set in concrete 1,400 years ago. The Muslim aim is foremost to make their divine law, the *Shar'iah*, the basic law for all the inhabitants of the earth. After that the right faith would be brought to the infidels. Even if those living in the 'abode of war' were not prepared to embrace Islam, they would have to live under the rule of the Muslims with *Shar'iah* as their constitution.

The terror attacks on 11 September, which bin Laden and his fundamentalist friends regarded as an act of holy war, were based on a *fatwa* (published decision on religious law recognised by an authority called *mufti*). It was not difficult for bin Laden to find a *mufti* willing to issue such a *fatwa* that gave the terrorists 'legal' warrant for the 'martyr actions'.

Suicide terrorists or martyrs?

The attacks on the USA on 11 September hit at the stronghold of capitalism and the military. It failed to hit the seat of democracy – or was the third target meant to be the White House? These were the most spectacular and successful attacks of the many that had so far been perpetrated under cover of holy war. The attacks were well planned. Their success was, for a great part, due to the fact that men and now even women are prepared to sacrifice themselves for the cause they believe is in Allah's interest.

Although suicide is forbidden in the Kor'an and the prophetic traditions, Muslims have other names for such heinous acts. They call them 'martyr actions' not suicide attacks or other names which the Western press uses. Those who sacrifice themselves in this way for the cause of Islam and Allah are regarded as martyrs. The Christian understanding of martyrdom, on the other hand, is when someone is killed because of his faith and lifestyle.

Islam and the Muslim *mullahs* promise the suicide attackers who are killed in action a divine acquittal of all transgression of the *Shar'iah* and unconditional access to Paradise. Furthermore the (male) martyr who is killed with the words of the Kor'an and the *Shahada* on his lips will, upon arrival in Paradise, be blessed with all its benefits. As mentioned, these include some fairly sensual relationships, often described vividly in erotic language, especially when these young men meet the 'black eyed' beauties (*Surah* 44:54; 55. 70).

In military and police strategies it is always taken for granted that the enemy, as far as possible, will do all he can to save his own life. Battle plans are made with that in mind. With suicide attacks the situation is completely different. The attackers have no plan to flee or save themselves. They have one supreme aim: to do as much damage to the enemy as possible without any consideration for their own security. Attacks that cannot be seen or heard create fear. And to spread fear is one of the main reasons for the attacks. This mind-set makes any form of defence against the suicide squads extremely difficult.

Western powers are talking about eliminating this kind of terror, this new type of war, and no doubt the superior technology at the disposal of modern armies will help to diminish unexpected assaults. But developed technology has not yet found an efficient way of fighting suicide bombers, because when one is killed there are many who are ready to take his or her place. And now the additional question of blood-revenge has become a primary motive.

chapter 10

Muslims in the West

For centuries Muslims and Christians in Western Europe were separated by the Mediterranean Sea and vast desert areas. Our forefathers heard about Muslims in the classroom when geography and history were on the timetable. Muslims, then, were that part of the world's population that did not count, that had no influence at all on the world outside the areas where they lived. Even there, their authority was generally only in matters that had to do with their religion. Most government and international affairs were in the hands of the European colonial powers.

Still, history reveals that there have always been significant interactions between Muslims in the Middle East and parts of Europe. We can divide these contacts into four different waves.

✱ First contact

The first wave of Muslims into Christian Europe took place around 711, less than a century after the death of the prophet. On that occasion the Moors, a North African people consisting of Berbers mixed with Arabs, conquered what today is Spain, Portugal and parts of Southern France. Sicily was put under the yoke of the Saracens, a nomadic people from the Syrian Desert. The Moors were more advanced in science and culture than Europeans in the Middle Ages. They left behind not only scientific works but also magnificent buildings. Three hundred years later, the Roman Catholics began to oust these intruders from European lands, but it was not until 1492 that the last Moors were driven from Spain. The Saracens left Sicily after 200 years.

✽ Second contact

The next wave of Muslims took place when hordes of Turks in the era of the Ottoman Empire overran Turkey's Western neighbours. In the sixteenth century this Empire stretched from Algeria to Iran, from Southern Russia to Yemen. Around 1,400 Turkish Muslims held sway over great areas in Eastern Europe – Albania, Bulgaria, Kosovo, Bosnia and segments of southern Russia. These areas, to some extent, remain Muslim and are creating problems for Europe today.

✽ Third contact

After the Second World War, and especially after 1950, we had the third wave, reaching into the very heart of Europe. Muslims came, however, were invited and came as immigrant workers. Germany and other European countries were experiencing a tremendous economic boom. This technological development resulted in an improved standard of living, but at the same time more effective family planning meant fewer children. People chose to enjoy affluence at the expense of raising children. The decreased population of Western Europe could not meet the demand for more people on the labour market. In order to meet this demand, Turks and Pakistanis and people from other countries with a surplus population were invited to help out. These invitations went generally to Muslim countries where religion was opposed to birth control. As most of these invited guest workers had no skills and minimal education, they took the simpler jobs in the manufacturing and service industries.

The immigrant labourers worked in the same conditions as anyone else. They had equal salary and enjoyed all the social benefits of European workers. The result was that when a period of unemployment occurred and the guest worker was sacked, he or she received full unemployment benefits. This meant a lot to them, as European unemployment benefits in most cases far exceeded full salary in their home countries. For that reason very few returned home when they had no jobs, were disabled or reached pensionable age. Their continued stay in Europe also brought with it the much-discussed reunion of families. To this must be added the fact that Muslim families in Europe generally have double the number of children compared with European families. These factors caused an increase in the Muslim populations in Europe, thus creating both cultural and economic problems.

* Fourth contact

The fourth wave of Muslims who migrated in the direction of Europe was the influx of refugees. There are many reasons for fleeing Muslim countries, even for the Muslims themselves. There is the enmity, and open war, between Jews and Palestinians. There are the almost permanent civil wars in Islamic (or part Islamic) nations such as the Sudan, Algeria, Somalia, Macedonia, Bosnia, and Kosovo. The war between Iraq and Iran caused many young men to flee to Europe to avoid military service. The Gulf War and the 'War Against Saddam' added their refugees.

In addition there are the numerous bloody conflicts between the two main branches of Islam, the Sunni and the Shi'ites. They not only fight each other; they also attempt to wipe out the smaller Muslim sects. Then there is the suppression and persecution of intellectual and well-educated Muslims in Pakistan and Iran. Hunger, floods, earthquakes and other natural disasters have caused people to flee their Muslim homelands to seek help in the Christian West. The multiple crises in Afghanistan have made a significant contribution to the number of refugees heading towards Europe.

These tragic events have also hit many of the Christian minorities who for centuries have been neighbours to Muslims, many of them for decades before Islam was introduced. The tragic fundamentalist negative currents have caused them to be the butt of persecution. They have been made landless and driven out of their homes in the Sudan, Pakistan and Indonesia, often with torture and executions taking place.

Economic refugees

To the thousands of refugees finding their way to Europe and North America we should add the many driven by the desire to have a better life. They have heard about the 'good life' enjoyed under Western governments and social legislation. Some claim all the social benefits almost as soon as they arrive. These 'refugees of convenience' have been known to use all methods — honest or dishonest — not only to cross borders, but also to manipulate the authorities in the nations into which they have found their way. Some, of course, have no valid reason for leaving their country of origin.

These refugees of convenience are not only a burden and extra expense for various governments; they are an embarrassment to the refugees who do have a justified reason for seeking asylum. Because of the way they exploit the welfare states of Western Europe they arouse disgust among their own people, as well as hurting the worthy needy.

Why the West?

The toilsome routes of Muslim refugees lead through both Islamic and Eastern European countries in order to reach their ultimate goal, Western Europe or North America. It would be logical for Muslims who flee Islamic countries for political or religious reasons to seek asylum in neighbouring Muslim nations. And that should not be impossible among the more than fifty nations in the world. For instance an Iraqi Shi'ite Muslim who was persecuted by Saddam Hussein could have fled across the border to Iran, which was not only a Shi'ite country, but also regarded as an enemy of Iraq.

But still, Christian countries — and especially the once 'Protestant' nations — are the ultimate goals. There are several reasons. Let us mention just two. The more essential is, no doubt, that these countries have the highest standard of living in the world. And the Western life-style is very attractive, the social benefits outstanding compared with the systems most refugees leave behind. Naturally they will choose places where the benefits are best.

Another reason for making the Western Christian world their final destination is that these countries treat people in distress in the same way as they treat their own citizens. No doubt this is very attractive to immigrants and draws many Muslims to our shores. Such treatment is unheard of in the developing world.

Muslims among Christians

Western Europe and North America have a history of hospitality towards persecuted peoples. Jews, Armenians and Huguenots have in general been able to settle well in their new countries.

Many Muslim groups and individuals, however, have problems. They do not settle well, and their lifestyle among Christians causes clashes of culture in many areas. While it is understandable and acceptable that people want to be faithful to the religion they grew up with, even when they choose to be citizens of another country, problems will arise when Muslims expect the strict demands of their religion as revealed in the Shar'iah law to be the norm for their chosen society and its people. It naturally causes offence when new immigrants expect their host's customs and culture to be changed to meet the needs of the special lifestyle of the Muslim.

The situation can in some ways be compared with that which the colonial powers created when European nations occupied exotic lands and introduced, sometimes even forced upon the people, Western languages, laws, customs, education systems and business methods, and at the same time exploited the people and natural resources.

Assimilation, integration, clashes of cultures

There are many changes of lifestyle for immigrants who have decided to settle in another country with different customs, religion and culture. We will briefly touch upon three:

Assimilation
The ideal will be assimilation, which is a process whereby a minority or immigrant group gradually adopts the characteristics of another culture, accepting the customs,

practices and lifestyle, even the religion, of the adopted country. The government, civil authorities and judicial systems are acknowledged. Of greatest importance is that the new language is learned. Most countries in Western Europe have outstanding examples of people who have been assimilated into a new culture.

Integration
Integration is the process whereby people unite with another culture in such a way as to become part of the adopted country. They are loyal to the government and authorities and live according to the laws. They learn the language of their new motherland while keeping their own religious convictions, some cultural traits and customs. The United States is an excellent example of successful integration of people from many races, cultures and religions.

Culture clash
Culture clash is a state of affairs where the host nation is expected to accept, and adjust society according to, the new immigrant's religion, culture and customs, which are often completely different. Many Muslims entering Western Christian countries have chosen this polarisation. The result has led not only to tensions, but confrontations, clashes and physical violence.

Elements of culture clash

In schools Muslims demand that special consideration be given to their children's dietary rules. Boys and girls have to be separated in the gym periods. Ideally they prefer girls and boys to be in different schools. They do not want girls and boys to socialise freely. They require public swimming baths to be reserved for Muslim women and children at certain times because Muslims should not go bathing with non-Muslims, especially people of the opposite sex. In hospitals it is expected that female doctors and nurses only treat Muslim women, who would be fed according to Muslim dietary rules. There have been instances in which Muslims have invited authorities to foot the bill for building mosques, Islamic culture centres and schools for Muslim children, where their parents' native language and the Kor'an have a prominent place in the timetable. There are also demands for Muslim cemeteries, which can create problems for following generations because a Muslim must remain undisturbed until 'the last day of history'. Christian cemeteries are often discontinued after 50-100 years.

Muslim practice can be followed without too many problems in Saudi Arabia, the cradle of Islam, where the various rules for the religion were introduced. The enormous uninhabited desert areas give plenty of space for tombs that can be kept for generations. In many Western countries such a practice would create problems within a few generations. Because of the need for agricultural land, it is already a dilemma in Muslim areas in India. The Hindus practise cremation as a religious rite, and there is no need for cemeteries.

Certain Muslim sects desire to conduct certain rituals at gravesides in connection with funerals. These practices can cause problems where cemeteries are generally closed at sunset.

Another reason for cultural confrontation is the ritual slaughtering of animals which takes place without anaesthesia during sacrifices in connection with certain Islamic festivals.

Culture clash and Shar'iah Law

The greatest and most visible confrontations between Christians and Muslims are caused by the demands and influence of the Shar'iah law. We have already dealt with this law and its dominant and outstanding influence not only in legal matters but also in the whole religious and private life of the Muslim.

Perhaps the most visible clash of all is the Shar'iah and cultural prohibition against contact or relationships with Christians and Christianity. The 'honour murders' committed by families against Muslim women who have Christian boyfriends are sad examples.

Child abduction

Child abduction is another issue. In the case of a divorce in an Islamic marriage, without a court case the father will automatically get custody of the children. This is Islamic law. And this, of course, is especially the case when the mother is a non-Muslim. It is the father's religious duty to make sure that the children are brought up according to Islamic principles.

It is preposterous to believe that the authorities, let alone the father in his native Muslim country, will respect a Western court order. No doubt the government authorities and police pay a lot of lip-service. They will try to please, but Islamic law makes it clear that the children belong to the father.

Law as a personal responsibility

The death penalty for rape, murder and apostasy from Islam, and the amputation of hands for theft are punishments that cannot be carried out in any Western country. There have, however, been some cases in which the family has taken the initiative and secretly and privately applied the strict Shar'iah punishments.

In this connection we should mention the circumcision of

girls. This inhuman and objectionable practice is prescribed neither in the Kor'an nor the prophetic traditions. It is not a law according to the Shar'iah. It is based solely on certain immigrants' local African culture. This does not stop societies accepting the ritual almost as a holy, religious decree.

In extreme cases some Muslims in Scandinavia have obtained citizenship in their country of choice and then made objections to paying respect to the national flag because it has the symbol of Christianity, the cross, in the centre. Some have even made protests regarding passports issued in European kingdoms because of the cross at the top of the royal coat of arms.

When in Rome, do as the Romans do

In my days as a missionary I resided in various Islam-dominated areas for some time. In general no real considerations were given to my Danish customs or Christian lifestyle. The unwritten rule was 'when in Rome, do as the Romans do'. In Western countries, however, Muslims demand privileges and rights they would never give to Christian guests in their own countries. They believe that Western laws really should be obeyed only when they are in agreement with the centuries-old Shar'iah law. In situations where Western law does not fulfil the strict requirements of the Islamic law, the Islamic law must be followed.

Juvenile delinquency

Perhaps the reason for the high rate of juvenile delinquency among second- and third-generation Muslim immigrants can be found in the fact that they live in two diverse worlds with systems of law that are very dissimilar. On the streets they are under Western law, which is rather liberal and grants them great freedom. In their homes they have parents who stand for principles influenced by the Koran and Islamic culture. The presence of these often inconsistent feelings and authorities will produce stress that can provoke a reaction in the form of rebellion against both home and society.

chapter 11
Reformation, coexistence

One thousand five hundred years after Christ, Christianity experienced a reformation, which was needed to meet new challenges. About 1,500 years have passed since Muhammad brought Islam onto the world scene. The questions, then, are: Is *Islam* now ready for a reformation? Is reformation possible?

The Christian Reformation is a much-discussed event. The 2,000-year history of Christianity has bloody chapters dealing with wars and lack of religious liberty, somewhat similar to the situations we hear about in certain Muslim countries today.

Conditions in many Islamic nations today can to some extent be compared with Christendom in the sixteenth century, when Martin Luther and the other reformers appeared on the world scene.

Corruption, poverty and humiliation

The time just before the Reformers came forward to proclaim their message was characterised by a corrupt papacy. The political systems were experiencing economic depression. The poorer Roman Catholic Christians suffered further by the various penances imposed on them by a greedy clergy. The effects of the Black Death, which a few decades before the Reformation had put more than one quarter of the population of Europe in their graves, could still be felt.

A great portion of Muslim dissatisfaction today is against the corrupt leaders in many Muslim nations and a religious system that does not adapt itself to the realities of modern times. Muslims are also embarrassed by Islamic sects fighting one another, not only with quotations from the Kor'an, but with arms. Perhaps the greatest reason for despair stems from the humiliation Muslims feel they are exposed to in so many ways from Western (Christian?) nations and Israel.

Science and economy

The Reformation was enhanced by two powerful influences from outside Europe.

The first, ironically, was the Arabs bringing the classical Greek literature – which they had preserved but which had been lost to Europe in the dark Middle Ages – back to its original status. At the same time, the Europeans took over the scientific progress that the Arabs had made while Europe 'slept' in the so-called 'Dark Ages'. It is interesting that our scientific triumphs which began 500 years ago had among other things Arabic research as an important basis. The other influence was the discovery of America, which brought some material riches to Europe. It was also the beginning of the colonial era.

Islam experiences a similar situation today. Oil supplies represent a material wealth from which many Islamic nations greatly benefit these days. This wealth makes it possible to buy Western technology and means of communication. A combination of oil and modern technique has a great potential for change – even reformation.

Osama bin Laden and Al-Qaida understood fully how to use modern technology in the attacks in the USA.

Dissatisfaction on the edges of the Islamic world

The Reformation did not take place at the centre of Christendom in the sixteenth century. Rome was not the place where it began. It happened in Bohemia, Switzerland, England and Germany.

The visible unrest among Muslims in the world today is not coming to the surface in Saudi Arabia. No doubt there is a lot of dissatisfaction with the way the royal family and the government there live up to the Muslim ideals. But in the country where the cradle of Islam stood, religion is used effectively to control the people. It is, however, at some distance from the centre, in Arab, Asian and North African Muslim countries where minds are in ferment. Dissatisfaction doesn't just smoulder under the surface, but is often expressed through direct acts of violence.

Could it be possible that a combination of these elements, which in Europe 500 years ago resulted in the Reformation that brought very positive changes among nations and peoples, could serve as a forerunner for a much-needed renewal in Islam?

History does not always repeat itself. Should we experience the much-needed Islamic reformation, we could hope that it would be one that would return to the original values. The Kor'an, with its words of respect for human beings, using no force in religion, and dialogue with persons of different religious convictions, would be an excellent platform for reform in Islam. This would be a start for religious liberty in the more than 50 Islamic nations. It could also lead to an improvement in standards of living for Muslims.

It seems, however, that an Islamic reformation along the lines of the Protestant Reformation in the sixteenth century is only wishful thinking.

Many young Muslims these days are convinced that violence directed towards Western Christian nations and against Israel is a significant part of the reformation and renewal so much needed and desired in Islam. After more than 300 years of apathy towards Western colonial domination and influence, it is felt that an Islamic reformation should take Muslims back to the original Islamic ideals revealed in the Kor'an and the Hadiths and enshrined in the *Shar'iah* law. The proposition has it, 'Our humiliations are due to the fact that we left the old paths and thereby have been disobedient to Allah's revealed will and plan for his people.' The perception is that the way forward is to fight against the powers that have hindered progress. Internally this means that corrupt Muslim leaders must be ousted from power. Externally, the 'great Satan' (USA and other Western Christian countries) must be fought against.

A thorough renewal in Islam could take place among Muslims who not only live in areas with religious liberty, but who have a background in religious liberty. The Afro-American Islamic societies could possibly play an important role in this rebirth of Islam into the twenty-first century. They live far away from the conservative centres and are in this way not so easily controlled by the conservative leaders.

Liberals and Fundamentalists

All religions have tensions among their liberals and fundamentalists. Both groups have basically the same aim, which is to strengthen and keep the faith under changing circumstances and the influences of modern society. Mention could be made of the strong influence of secularism on all religions. However, to reach their goals they use quite different means. The Muslim fundamentalist will go back in history, argue and even fight to revive and re-introduce the simple undiluted faith and lifestyle of the pioneers. On the other hand, the liberals believe that in order for their religion to survive in modern society it must be reinterpreted without losing its uniqueness and be able to meet the demands and questions of modern times.

The liberals are facing the hardest challenge. Study and consideration are necessary in order to persuade anyone to change.

The task for the fundamentalist is simple. The approach to the issues is direct and uncomplicated. The Kor'an and the Hadiths are considered law in Islam. The *Shar'iah* must be followed. Every word in the Kor'an originates with Allah and should be obeyed without condition or interpretation.

All religions have adherents who have only a rudimentary grasp of their theology. That highlights the greatest danger for Muslims living among Christians. Those Muslims in 'Christian' lands who have only a minimal knowledge of Islam are tempting and easy targets, and vulnerable to the simplistic solutions and exploitation of fundamentalist groups working among them.

Is coexistence at all possible?

September 11 has changed the world much more than we recognise. Even the men who planned the attacks did not foresee all the consequences. The terrorists harvested some unexpected and undeserved profit from their fight against the Christian West. In addition to the damaging effect on the world of finance, air traffic, security systems, unemployment, and military strategies, the attacks increased hostilities between people. Muslims and Christians are today more suspicious and hostile towards one another than ever. All over the world the event has created tension and fear in both camps.

On a local level, where Muslims and Christians had lived together in peace and harmony, they are now watchful, suspicious and hesitant towards one another. The situation confirms people in their fears. Political parties and organisations with strong nationalistic programmes are gaining ground. Limitations on the number of immigrants allowed into the country and restrictions on their rights and privileges are discussed. In some countries, young fanatics from both sides often meet on the streets in direct confrontation.

Confrontations are also taking place among the Muslims themselves, especially where they are in a minority among Christians. Extremist Muslim groups who accept the suicide attacks – those that took place in the United States with great loss of life and the many in Israel – are challenging more peace-loving fellow-believers to support a hard line. Muslim immigrants, guest workers and refugees are provoked openly to declare that they agree with and are prepared to participate in the 'holy war'.

Among Christians in various denominations there is a tendency towards polarisation. Here there are – in certain cases – additional reasons for the more radical extremist positions. Some conservative evangelical Christians in North America and Europe believe that Israel is still the object of special blessings from God. Such an interpretation of certain passages in the Bible has a tendency to push humanitarian considerations into the background, allowing a subjective religious fanaticism to determine the agenda. Whatever Israel does, they argue, it is in accordance with God's plan and for that reason cannot be wrong. Christians of other traditions, including those actually represented in Israel, take a more humanitarian, pro-Palestinian stance. Christians in both traditions, however, are apt to be more than a little concerned about the impact of Islam and Islamic peoples in once-Christian Western societies. Negative feelings towards immigrants and refugees on the part of secular 'Christians' are not a new phenomenon. September 11 and other atrocities in which Muslims were involved have simply intensified these negative feelings.

What about the future?

As mentioned, Muslims live in an integrated society. Rules regarding religion, marriage and family life, culture and customs, politics, diet and many other issues are scrupulously dictated by the Kor'an and the Hadith and set in concrete in the Shar'iah law. Entrance to the Islamic Paradise is possible only by the strictest obedience to these rules and injunctions. Yet there *is* room for the odd exception.

The Shar'iah law can be observed only in a Muslim country

In Islam it is not possible to make a clear line of demarcation between the religious and the secular. Such a worldview, which Muslims believe has its origin with Allah, has wide-ranging consequences, because it means that the sincere Muslim can really live and operate only in an area in which the Shar'iah is the universal and absolute law and guide for both government and personal life. Such a religious outlook also means that the true Muslim, wherever he lives, has to do all he can to ensure that the Shar'iah will be introduced as the basic and fundamental law. Only where that is the case is he able to be a true Muslim.

It is obvious, then, that a true Muslim, whose salvation

depends more on obedience to the rules of the Shar'iah than to the grace of Allah, will not be able to practise his religion fully in any Western (Christian) society.

We will mention just a few examples. In Western society the inheritance of daughters and sons tends to be equal. According to the Shar'iah, daughters can lay claim to only half of what the sons inherit. In a Muslim courtroom one man's evidence equals that of two women. In a Western bank a person is paid dividends for investments and has to pay interest for loans. Any form of interest *(Riba)* is forbidden in Islamic law. A Western divorce court may reject accusations of unfaithfulness and adultery. In Western countries the Muslim is continually tempted by women on the streets and will have to walk with his eyes lowered, as almost all the women he sees are not dressed according to Islamic codes of chastity. According to the Kor'an he has no right to look at them.

In Western Christian countries there is religious liberty. People are allowed to change their religion. This means that should the sincere Muslim's children choose to be Christians they are protected by the law. In Islam there is the death penalty for becoming a Christian, or for that matter conversion to any other religion. In Western society the young women have the right to choose their own partners, who may well be Christians. A Muslim woman has no right to marry a Christian, but a Muslim man *can* marry a Christian or Jewess.

In an interview, Osama bin Laden said, no doubt on the basis of the above mentioned and other prohibitions, 'Muslims should not live in the land of the infidels for a long time.' To the Muslim who desires to live according to Islamic rules, these Western (Christian) laws, customs and regulations will remain constant stumbling blocks to his practising his religion fully. As Islam is a rather legalistic religion, where admission to Paradise is conditional upon a scrupulous obedience to the law, a prolonged stay in a Christian country, with all the temptations it incurs, would be a hindrance. With this background one has to understand the Islamic worldview that asserts that Muslims who live in non-Islamic societies must strive for the introduction of Islamic laws. This is not only the criterion for being a good Muslim and the condition for entering Paradise; it is also the main method of spreading the Islamic faith. Muslims think that the requirements and tenets of the Shar'iah are so logical and convincing that they will promote Islam in a positive way and make people convert to Islam. For these reasons, the fundamentalist will fight for the cause.

There are Muslims and Muslims

There is no doubt that the majority of Muslims living among Christians want peace and tolerance. They prefer a relaxed relationship with their Christian neighbours and fellow-workers. They appreciate the liberty they possess in Western society, and welcome the possibilities for the work and income they enjoy. They are grateful for the benefits and securities which the social legislation generally ensures to all within the borders of a Christian country. The 'first generation' immigrants, guest workers and refugees remember the conditions that were prevailing in many of the Muslim countries they left behind.

This positive majority group, perhaps more than 90% of the Muslims among the Christians, are generally well accepted. Many of them are an asset to our societies and bear their burden in our industries and business world. The question, however, is whether they are 'good' Muslims in their meaning of the word, and in the evaluation of their more fundamentalist brothers and sisters. Do they live up to the rigid standards of Islam? They are living in a Christian society where the laws generally do not meet the strict requirements of the Shar'iah. For this reason they are really not able to be Muslims to perfection. They are living in the land of the infidels with all its temptations.

The other group among the Muslims in Western countries constitutes perhaps less than 10%. These are the more radical, with fundamentalist tendencies. Although they constitute a small minority they are very active. They are loud, aggressive, ready to fight and therefore very visible. They take advantage of the freedom to speak and act granted by most Western societies. Unchallenged by the authorities, and protected by the police, they can publicly express their ideas and opinions on even the most controversial subject matter. They enjoy a freedom that would not be granted them in their Muslim home countries. It is usually the second or third generation of immigrants who behave in this way. They have not themselves experienced conditions in the countries of their ancestors. They have not generally understood the reasons for immigration, but they fully accept the idea that when living in the land of war *(Dal al Harb)* it is the faithful Muslim's religious duty to do all he can with all his power to fight for the spread of Islam, the true faith.

That means first of all to get the *Shar'iah* introduced. Not only are they called to challenge the laws, customs, culture and religion of their host country; they must also take every opportunity to seek confrontations with more relaxed fellow Muslims who in their opinion do not live up to the Islamic ideals. And those more carefree Muslims, the majority, are reasonably satisfied with the status quo.

Theoretically they live in the 'land of war', but in practice they exist in the 'land of peace'.

It is in this area that we have to be watchful. The number of Muslims in the West grows with amazing speed. Statistics today are outdated tomorrow. The growth is not only a result of new immigrants. It is perhaps more because birth control is an un-Islamic practice. Statistics today are outdated tomorrow.

The conflict between the Shar'iah and Western lifestyle

Many Muslims who have arrived in Christian countries are assets. Together with the indigenous population they help keep things moving. And, like their hosts, the majority want to live in peace. No doubt many give only lip-service to the most important Islamic rituals and beliefs. As one young Muslim expressed it: 'We want to be Muslims in the same way as the younger generation of Christians are Christians. They celebrate Easter and Christmas. We will take part in the significant Muslim festivals. The rest of the time we will enjoy life the same way our "Christian" friends do.'

The problems arise when fanatical and extreme minorities feel they are called to police the many in order to enforce their perfect obedience. The demands of the *Shar'iah* compel its adherents not only to proclaim Islam but also to fight for the spread of Islam in *Dar el-Harb* (the 'land of war') – perceived by them as their great mission. This is one of the reasons why they have left *Dar el-Islam* ('the land of peace').

Rabid Muslims can intimidate by threats or the severe punishments outlined in the Shar'iah as a means of persuasion. Apostasy from and renunciation of Islam mean capital punishment. Facing such consequences, nominal

Muslims will in most cases, perhaps a little reluctantly, take sides with more extreme fellow Muslims. They will also feel obliged to take a stand for Islam as the only true religion to ensure its propagation by all means, and to make people acknowledge that obedience to the Shar'iah law is an expression of Allah's purpose for all nations and races.

As Christians we believe that the Kingdom of God is a phenomenon taking place inside the believer. In Islam it is understood that the rule of Allah begins here on earth with a government based on principles from the Kor'an and Islamic laws. In other words, the environment around the Muslim should also be in accordance with the purposes of Allah.

From the accepted writings in Islam, the fundamentalist is able to interpret certain texts from the Kor'an, and citations from the Hadith, to mean that Islam is the only true religion, Muhammad the last prophet, and the *Shar'iah* an expression of Allah's will as the constitution for all people on earth. The conclusion of course is that it is not only the call of each Muslim but also his *duty* to fight by all means for the introduction of this religion all over the world. Only when Shar'iah is ruling in his surroundings is he able to be a true follower of Islam. When he is in a Christian land, Allah has arranged for his being there with the sole purpose of obeying Allah's call.

With the methods and arms Muslims have been prepared to employ in various situations, it is obvious that a small minority of rabid Muslims can be a real threat in days to come – even in a peaceful Christian country.

Hope – perhaps

Christians and Muslims make up more than half of the world's population. In the teachings of both religions the peace concept has a prominent place. Christ is called the Prince of Peace, and Muslims greet one another with the words *'assalam alaikum'* – peace be unto you. The word Islam means surrender. It has its root in the Arabic words for peace and salvation. One of the 99 names of Allah is *'assalam'*, meaning The Peace.

Extremists in both the Christian and the Muslim camps often make this peace concept void. And it is no doubt easier for the Muslim to find in the Kor'an and the Hadiths, as they are interpreted, and in the *Shar'iah* law justification for violent attacks in religious wars when he lives in the 'land of war', a Christian country. Texts in the Old Testament that could be interpreted as justification for violence in the defence of religion, even ethnic cleansing, have been neutralised by the teaching of the later prophets and the love principle culminated in the example and words of Jesus. In the history of the Bible and the Christian Church one discovers that various awakenings resulted in better conditions for mankind and peace among warring peoples.

In the Kor'an the Muslim will also find support for peaceful coexistence with, and mutual respect for, people of other faiths.

One of the briefer *Surahs* (109:1-6) suggests that even when a Muslim cannot accept the way a non-Muslim worships, he must be prepared to accept other people's rights to their own religion and manner of worship. The authorised introduction to this *Surah* and the resumé of the texts explain that the Muslim who has the truth naturally cannot follow false doctrines. In the same way, the non-Muslim will not abandon his heresies. This *Surah*, which was probably written in Mecca, accepts the right of others even to reject Islam. A Muslim should show them the right way and try to persuade them to accept Islam. However, all people have the right to pursue other religions. There is no valid reason to persecute or attack other people on account of religion. The most well-known text in this connection is *Surah* 2:256, where we read that there should be no compulsion in religion.

The problem with coexistence is that fundamentalists in both camps are using certain texts in isolation as a support for their attacks. Their influence should be curtailed, but that can be done only by education and information. Dialogue is not only possible and desirable; it is a necessity. In the world today there are enormous possibilities for meaningful co-operation between Christians and Muslims on such topics as human rights, religious liberty, and assistance to refugees and the millions of people suffering from starvation and disease.

chapter 12

A Christian meets a Muslim

Most Muslims who have migrated to the West, for whatever reasons, are here to stay. Many have obtained citizenship. The controversial debate about the future of immigrants and the support of the many refugees is high on the agenda of politicians and parliaments.

Professing Christians have conflicting feelings in this debate. On the one hand there is a great fear for how things will develop with the ever-growing number of Muslims. Many of them are very visible owing to the colour of their skin, their language and their lifestyle. Many of them are rather noisy and do not really fit into our culture pattern. They are perceived as a threat to our Western Christian culture and our way of living. On the other hand it is a Christian duty to help all who are suffering. The parable of the Good Samaritan lays on the Christian a duty to help all in need, irrespective of culture and race. Jesus said that each should love his neighbour as himself. There is no doubt that these words are the foundation of the generous social laws the West has developed.

The same biblical principles of love and concern are embedded in the ten commandments, when it is prescribed in the law about the day of rest and worship, that the 'stranger within your gates' is also expected to be included in the blessings of the Sabbath. We have to remind ourselves that Egypt, today a country in the centre of Islam, on at least three occasions saved God's chosen people in the Old Testament, when they were persecuted or suffered hunger and starvation.

The Great Commission

Christians who are serious in their worship and practice have in the last 300 years been engaged in missionary activities. The Great Commission in Matthew 28, where the church is commanded to go out into the entire world to proclaim the Gospel, has been taken to heart. When Christ asked his followers to go and proclaim 'the everlasting gospel', he had all the inhabitants of the world in mind, 'every nation, tribe, language and people' (Rev. 14: 6). And in general the results have been outstanding. Continents that 200 years ago did not have a reasonable knowledge of the Christian message are now leaders in Christian outreach and have ever-growing church families or groups.

Mission in Muslim lands

There are, however, areas where Christian missions have had very little impact and progress, countries where Christian churches have hardly gained a foothold. Islam, being a world-religion in its own right, has been extremely resistant to the Christian Gospel. This in spite of the fact that many years of missionary work in Muslim countries and among their people have taken place. Many missionaries have been sent to Muslim countries at great expense, but the result of their earnest work has been meagre.

What was called 'world mission' is enjoying a new day, however. People of the world now live in a 'global village'.

We have new and interesting neighbours, many of whom are Muslim. These new conditions have opened up Christian witnessing possibilities to people who belong to that sixth part of the world population which is almost untouched by the Christian message. One quarter of Muslims, about 300 million, live in circumstances outside their Muslim home countries where Christians can freely meet them, associate with them, and in this way witness to their Christian faith. The other 900 million live in about 50 nations where contact with them is difficult if not impossible.

Where Muslims are resistant to Christianity, even refusing to listen to the Christian viewpoint, there are theological, historical and sociological reasons. The most important could well be the laws that limit religious liberty in Islamic nations, with the threat of execution for leaving Islam.

Unsuccessful mission among Muslims in Christian nations

It is a fact that Western Christians, with their comprehensive laws of religious liberty, have not really been able to make meaningful contact with the Muslims in their midst. The death penalty for apostasy from Islam cannot, of course, be carried out in a Western country. However, group pressure from both the family and Muslim society is always present and social exclusion is distressing.

The reason Muslims in our midst do not feel a need for what Christianity has to offer could be that Muslims generally have no, or very little, respect for the way Christianity is practised by 'Christians' in Western countries. More often than not, they have problems with the *way* Christians live than with the *tenets of the Christian faith*. The moral degeneration in so-called 'Christian' countries is interpreted by Muslims as proof that as a religion with influence on its adherents' lifestyle Christianity has gone bankrupt. And we have to admit that this too often appears to be the case.

Muslims observe the free and open association between men and women, the easy access to pornography, use of alcohol, abuse of drugs and offensive TV programmes. No doubt Muslims have great admiration and respect for the social concern they meet, both in health and in sickness. But even in these areas they find that there is a hidden brutality and carelessness in the way we treat elderly people in society. We leave them lonely in nursing homes with few visits by the near family.

Christians tend to have little contact with Muslim neighbours, and rarely show strangers among them much friendliness, let alone hospitality. These virtues, the essence of Christian (and also Muslim) being, are in many cases the most efficient tools to open up communication and integration. But those who look different and are dressed differently are often met with indifference and treated coldly, even with hostility. Generally, Western people are not over-friendly to one another, and strangers are kept at a distance.

Such attitudes strengthen Muslims in their culture clash and incite them unconsciously to erect various protective 'iron curtains' around themselves. In this way they isolate themselves and are further removed from the influence of the Gospel. Muslim imams use this as an effective warning against Christians and their message. In spite of these obstacles we have to admit that the possibilities of bringing the Gospel to Muslims today are quite different. What used to be termed a mission field, across the waters and deserts, is now neighbour-evangelism. What was regarded as a dangerous and expensive enterprise is now a call to witness to neighbours and workmates.

Muslims among us are in a state of transition

The Muslims in our countries are accessible as they live in a free country. And they are, at least at the beginning of their stay, in a transitional period. They are uncertain of their future, and new impressions make them open to new ideas and concepts. This is especially the case with first-generation immigrants. They have left family and friends. They have to face the new challenges in their places of work. The climate, smells and food are different. Their support in the Islamic religion has also changed. Now they face the challenge of building a new existence among people who have another religion, speak another language and have different cultures and customs.

Our Muslim neighbours are freed from the direct pressures they were previously exposed to by society. They are in a kind of intermediate station, away from the usual conditions in their native countries. The new things they experience are exciting, but also disconcerting. These factors make them open and ready to change course in their lives. They are seeking solutions to their new problems and guidance in an unknown future. This makes them open to suggestions and perhaps more ready to listen to the Christian witness. In this state of transition they are responsive to new challenges.

When the Christian message is presented in such situations — in an honest and understandable way and accompanied by Christian love and concern — it will fill the vacuum that all immigrants are bound to experience.

Variable attitudes

As we have said previously, we need to remember that there are various kinds of Muslims. As we have stated, they are divided into different sects in the same way as there are many sects among Christians. Islam is not a solid block of believers, and not all Muslims practise their religion in the same way. Religion means different things to different people. They come from more than 1,000 culture groups with their own individual customs and languages. There are Muslims who are fundamentalist and those who take a more liberal stand. There are Muslims who want to turn the clock back and live the way they lived at the time of Muhammad, while other Muslims desire to adapt their religion to modern times and make their religion relevant to the twenty-first century.

It is not possible to list all the attitudes to life, culture, and customs among Islamic people. A Turkish guest worker will differ in many ways from a student from Algeria. A farmer from Pakistan will not have much in common with a businessman from Indonesia. Even their outlook on Islam will be disparate. Some will follow a line from the fundamentalist orthodox, believing in the verbal inspiration of the Kor'an, following all the traditions in detail, and organising their lives in accordance with the strict injunctions from the *Shar'iah*. On the other hand there are the conservative Muslims, who attempt to follow the rules, especially when it comes to the Five Pillars, while working for a modernisation of the *Shar'iah* to fit into the twenty-first century. Then on the left wing are the liberals, who consent to only a few of the strict rules and even render tolerant interpretations of these.

Between the most extreme points we find the *Sufis* (mystics) who seek a special connection with the divine; the *syncretists* who intermix Islamic beliefs and practice with various kinds of superstitions not in alignment with orthodox Islamic teachings; and the secular who are only Muslims by name and who, for social, political or personal reasons have shelved most of the rules and customs.

The religious and social conditions portrayed in this book are more or less common to Muslims, irrespective of their culture or sectarian affiliations and whether they live in traditional Islamic countries or as 'Diaspora' (foreigners) in the West.

Though they can be different in their observance of religion and in lifestyle, Muslims have one thing in common – in the early days of their exile they are open to new ideas and impressions. Here are some suggestions on how to meet, develop friendships, and even dialogue on religious themes with Muslims.

Friendship

Genuine friendship is the most important condition for establishing a good and amiable relationship with a Muslim. First of all there must be some personal contacts. It is of utmost importance that mutual confidence and understanding is brought about as a valid foundation for meaningful communication. They have the same joys and sorrows, burdens, fears, hopes and failures as other people. They have weaknesses to overcome in the same way as Christians do.

Friendliness is not always easy for a Western person, who tends to assess people before having dealings with them.

An appreciation expressed for a favour or a courtesy, a friendly word for a service, a helping hand, an apology when the situation requires it, and a spontaneous attempt to have a conversation are all positive factors which will help to establish friendship and communication. These are steps in the direction of meaningful friendships that will help in integration and in the playing down of unpleasant cultural clashes.

Immigrants, refugees and guest workers have in many situations been exposed to the positive influence that the Christian religion has had on society and the social welfare laws they also enjoy. But it may also be the case that the 'stranger within our gates' has seldom experienced practical Christianity from those who profess to be followers of Jesus Christ. Christianity lived out in life would make a Muslim convert to Christianity in only a very few cases, but it would create a respect for the Christians and thereby promote the slow process of integration.

Knowledge and information

Another important factor in making friends and gaining respect is the need to have an elementary knowledge of the religion of Islam, its belief system, rituals, rules and regulations. Information relating to the home country of our Muslim friend is also a must. Christ used these significant areas when he met the Samaritan woman (John 4). By asking her to do him a favour, requesting a drink of water, before he engaged in his witnessing activities, he put himself in the role of the receiver, made himself a debtor to her, enabling her to keep her dignity. Her role was to be a generous giver and not a humble listener and receiver. This principle is of extreme significance in both our social work and outreach activities.

Hospitality

Hospitality is, without doubt, the surest way to a Muslim's heart. Hospitality is an important part of the Islamic culture, a positive virtue. Among Arabs, when a friendship has been established they will say 'there is salt between us', which means, we have eaten together and are friends.

The act of accepting an invitation to eat together is saying yes to friendship, and one of the most effective means of breaking down prejudice. Hospitality is a two-way street: usually it begins with an invitation from the Christian. He or she represents the host country. Then he accepts an invitation to the home of the Muslim.

Consideration must be given to the special diet of Muslims. Also it must be remembered that any relationship between the opposite sexes is a sensitive area. The frankness of the West in such connections – even those we think are most innocent – is easily misunderstood and judged as superficial and immoral. As a good rule it is recommended that men cultivate friendship with men and women with women. In a family situation there is generally more openness. Muslim families can be freer in a social relationship with other families.

Listen and learn

Listen to your Muslim contact. He or she is both willing and prepared to talk about his or her religion. It is, perhaps, not recommended that we engage in discussion on doctrines in which Christians and Muslims differ, until a mutual relationship of trust has been established. There are areas of doctrinal conflict where Muslims are not allowed to listen to criticism. The Muslim has no right to discuss divisive issues relating to Allah, Muhammad and the Kor'an.

By listening one will learn not only about Islam but also about the Muslim friend's personal attitude towards his religion.

One also has to be an *honest* listener. When the Muslim mentions faults and mistakes in the way Christianity is practised in the West, one should not try to defend the indefensible. Honestly admit it when he is right or has a valid point.

Personal conversations

Personal conversations are more important than group discussions. Invitations to attend church or Christian meetings should not take place before a natural and relaxed friendship has been established. Although Muslims in our countries live in societies with religious freedom, they will always be under group pressure from concerned fellow Muslims. Family and fellow compatriots observe them constantly. With their strong ties of solidarity they will not only observe the doings and goings of one another. They will also monitor non-Muslim activities, attitudes and friends.

In all conversations it must be remembered that Islam is not only a religion with beliefs and rituals. It is the guide to their whole existence. The Muslim is not just a part of his family. He is part of the Islamic nation as well as the worldwide community. The extreme individualism we experience among Western people is not accepted by Muslims and is not appreciated. The witness of the Christian faith can convince a Muslim, but it is still extremely difficult, and could prove fatal, to change his religion. Even in countries with religious liberty it is always wise for a Muslim who converts to Christianity to obtain permission from, or at least inform, the family before taking such an important step. Alternatively, he could choose to be a Christian in secrecy by taking another identity.

The extended family

Any persuasive dialogue, preferably conducted in private, will accomplish most and protect the Muslim interested in Christianity from pressure from both the family and the group. Also here it is advisable, whenever possible, that dominant members of the family know what is going on.

Should a person take a stand to be a Christian, the pastor in charge must be sure that the new convert is able and strong enough to stand up against subsequent boycotting, isolation and even more serious threats. These can be expected not only from the Islamic society, but also from the extended family. There are tragic cases, even in Western countries, where family members have carried out executions.

Loss of face can mean loss of faith

As mentioned, the Christian is counselled to avoid discussions on doctrinal differences until a relaxed friendship has been established. Admittedly, in a religious dialogue with Muslims a point will sooner or later come when confrontations are unavoidable. It must always be remembered that in Eastern culture it is not only embarrassing but humiliating to lose face. When one is able to meet arguments with more convincing arguments one must always make sure that the Muslim opponent is never ridiculed nor humiliated. It can be tempting to win an argument, but it can easily result in losing a friend. This is certainly the case when the discussion takes place in the presence of other people. In such cases Christians must be 'as wise as serpents'.

Avoid criticism

A conversation with a Muslim can easily develop into a discussion of the relative advantages in Christianity compared with Islam, Christ with Muhammad, the Bible with the Kor'an. Generally such debates are futile. The Christian should carry a positive testimony of his belief in Jesus. Comments and criticisms of Islamic conditions and standings, such as their prophet's conduct, the strict punishment for transgressing the Shar'iah law, the morals of individual

Muslims or their religious rituals will in general fall outside conversations of these kinds. When a conversation turns to talk about the individual person's lack of principle, worldly lifestyle and abuse of religion, neither Christian nor Muslim should have anything to say. There are weak adherents in both camps.

Dialogue on sensitive issues cannot in the long run be avoided. However, a direct confrontation should not take place until a solid platform of mutual trust with respect, tolerance, and indulgence has been built. Such discussion should take place in a spirit of objectivity, honesty and reliability.

Dreams as part of a Muslim's religious experience

Dreams and their meanings have great significance in the lives of many Muslims. This is especially the case in the religious sphere. From earliest history dreams have played a major role as the basis for important decisions in life. And in Islamic cultures today great emphasis is put on things that have been revealed to people in dreams.

In Bible history dreams also played a vital part. There are references to dreams and visions as tools in the hand of God – the means God used to communicate with people in certain circumstances.

Muslims in general have a positive outlook on dreams. They will readily tell of situations where they were guided by dreams. This is an area where Christians should at least learn to take these supernatural matters seriously, even if they cannot fully understand them.

chapter 13

Christian and Muslim beliefs

As mentioned, an elementary knowledge of the faith of Muslims is of the greatest importance if a meaningful dialogue between the two religions is to take place. In previous chapters the *Shar'iah* law, the role of the prophet in Islam, the importance and sacredness of the Kor'an, Muslim rituals and ceremonies, the dietary laws and the Muslim lifestyle have been discussed in some detail. The Muslim understanding of the end of time and the role of angels has just been touched upon.

In this chapter we will detail a few of the most essential Islamic beliefs. We should be cautioned that the various tenets of faith in the world's religions cannot be paralleled. The same words and concepts can mean quite different things in the two religions.

The areas where conceptual misunderstandings are most apparent are on the question of God, Allah and Jesus Christ, which naturally touch on the most important doctrines in both religions. These issues are important in all religions, and we find the greatest differences between Christianity and Islam.

The Sovereign Allah

Christians teach and believe that there is one Godhead —

Father, Son and Holy Spirit. It is a unity of three eternal persons, called the Trinity. God the Father is the Creator, source and upholder of all creation. God, the eternal Son, was incarnated in Jesus Christ. He created all things. By his vicarious death, Jesus became the Saviour of the world. God, the Holy Spirit, draws men and women to God and bestows spiritual gifts on the Church.

Muslims teach that there is no other god but Allah. Allah is unique and *one*. He has neither children nor partners. He is creator and upholder. He controls everything. Allah created men and women, but not in his image. At first glance one could get the impression that the God in Christianity and the Allah in Islam are the same person. Or at least there is a significant overlapping. However, this similarity is only apparent. When a Christian talks about his God, the concept of the Trinity is included. To the Muslim this is blasphemous. Allah is one. The idea of 'three in one' is profanity.

The ninety-nine names of Allah

The attributes of Allah are revealed in the 99 most significant names that have been ascribed to him. In these names he is designated as being holy, merciful, forgiving, protecting, omniscient and almighty. At the same time, it is worth noting that among the names of Allah are also some which tell of his using force, that he conquers, degrades, humiliates, retards, revenges and does damage. As mentioned earlier, three of the most important names showing our God's positive relationship to mankind are missing from Allah's 99, for in Islam, Allah is never called love, father, or a spirit.

Allah is one. To Muslims, Jesus Christ is only 'an honoured prophet'. He is also called 'the spirit of Allah, a special attribute to Isa' (Jesus). The same attribute is given to Adam. The Spirit in Islamic theology is not an independent person in the deity.

In regard to the argument that adherents of the two religions are virtually worshipping the same God (Allah) there are, no doubt, many parallels, and these similarities are excellent points on which to meet. However, it is in the doctrine of the Trinity where the greatest difference is to be found. The core of the Christian faith that the one and only God exists in three persons (Father, Son and Holy Spirit) in one Godhead, is completely misunderstood by many Muslims and unacceptable to all.

As Christians we do not claim a full understanding of the Trinity. It is a mystery that cannot be understood. It is accepted in faith.

Predestination

There are other essential differences in understanding the God of the Bible and the Allah of the Kor'an which should be recognised. Islam believes in an almighty god, Allah. All people have to submit to his will. Allah is immeasurably different from humans. Attributes ascribed to him may not be compared in any way with human characteristics. Allah is self-sufficient. He cannot in any way be affected or influenced by human beings and their actions. He is the source of all things both good and evil. His will is supreme and not limited by laws or principles.

The natural result of such an understanding of the deity is fatalism. Many times a day Muslims express the word, *'Insha'llah'* (it is the will of Allah). In Islam, Allah and his purposes and plans are not and cannot be known by men.

In contrast to this belief in predestination, Christians believe that in Christ God made himself known to men and women (John 1:18). He has revealed himself to mankind. Men and woman were created in his image (Genesis 1:27). This Christian understanding is in sharp contrast to the Islamic concept of Allah's 'otherness'. The Christian God is closer to his people. He is concerned and loving.

There are other decisive differences. In Islamic understanding Allah's power is revealed in grandeur, and in political and military superiority. The prophet Muhammad was also a military commander and statesman. In Christian understanding, although God is almighty, on occasions he reveals his omnipotence in weakness, humility and suffering. Calvary is a revelation of God's endless love made visible in the humanity of Christ. This contrast is vividly illustrated when we consider that the prophet Muhammad fled the holy city (Mecca) when danger threatened him. In Christianity the Saviour of the world volunteered to *enter* the holy city (Jerusalem) to die for his people.

Jesus Christ

In his life of obedience to God, his suffering, death and resurrection, Jesus brought salvation to mankind. This was the only way to atone for the sins of men and women. All who believe and accept this sacrifice and atonement will receive everlasting life.

In Islam, Jesus *(Isa)* is honoured as one of the greatest, if not the greatest, of the prophets. Allah used him, but he was not divine. Jesus is mentioned 93 times in the Kor'an. Muslims believe in the virgin birth. Christ is called 'the spirit of Allah', 'the word of Allah', but he is not honoured as the Son of God.

Muslims mock and accuse Christians of having *three* gods: the Father (God), the Son (Jesus Christ) and the mother (Mary). As stated elsewhere this flagrant misinterpretation of one of the most fundamental dogmas in Christianity results in Muslims accusing Christians of being polytheists. They even go so far as to accuse Christians of worshipping an immoral god who had a relationship with a woman. This coarse accusation and serious misinterpretation by the ignorant has caused many bitter misunderstandings. It should, however, be added that an enlightened Muslim does not take this stand.

The Kor'an designates Christ as 'Allah's prophet and witness'. It even states that Christ is the one nearest to Allah, the righteous one, and the messenger. The Kor'an even mentions some miracles performed by Christ. The title Messiah is ascribed to Christ. It is, however, difficult to determine how that title is understood and what it implies to the Muslim believer. In the Kor'an, Christ has a high status and is honoured by Muhammad. But the prophet of Islam never acknowledged Jesus as being divine. The Hadith (Traditions), collected more than 200 years after the death of Muhammad, actually toned down the role, status and importance of Christ.

Christ in Islam is not the second person of the Godhead. He was not crucified, but rather taken to heaven by Allah. There is no need of a Saviour in Islam. Salvation is obtained by surrendering to Allah's will. Do the right deeds and live in accordance with the Five Pillars and the *Shar'iah*, and salvation and access to Paradise is the potential result. For that reason there is no need for an atoning sacrifice. A Muslim believes works save him.

However, even if a Muslim is able to be obedient and faithful to all rules, rituals and laws in Islam, he has no *guarantee* of entrance to paradise. The Muslim will also use the *'insha'llah'* (it is the will of Allah) in this connection. These words are used to express that all the plans and relationships of men are completely subject to Allah's will which is believed to be just but perhaps somewhat unpredictable. A Muslim can be faithful and live fully in accordance with all the requirements of Islam, but this does not necessarily give him access to paradise. Muslim theology claims that if obedience could secure paradise, man would be able to 'manipulate' Allah into saving the faithful person, and Allah is beyond any form of manipulation. Even after a long life of scrupulous submission, the Muslim can be granted entrance to paradise only if Allah decides it *(insha'llah)*. An individual cannot *claim* the privilege.

The essential differences in the concept of the deity in Islam and Christianity have a decisive influence on people's perception of sin and how a person is saved.

The concept of sin

Muslims and Christians agree that Adam was disobedient and for that reason had to leave the Garden of Eden. Islam, however, teaches that the fall did not make any changes in Adam's nature. Allah forgave Adam and he was reinstated. Adam and the succeeding generations, according to Muslim teaching, were not weakened by the fall. Men and women are not believed to be sinful by nature. They are rather regarded as being weak, ignorant and forgetful.

These contending perceptions of sin and salvation in Christianity and Islam are probably the greatest stumblingblocks for a Muslim to overcome before he can accept Christianity. Central to this vital issue is acceptance or rejection of Jesus Christ as Saviour.

In Islam sin is divided into three categories:

1. Some sins are just mistakes, misunderstandings or instances of neglect. The consequences of these kinds of sins are sanctions rather than punishments.

2. Other sins are more serious transgressions and will entail punishments. Mentioned in this category can be disobedience to parents, murder of a fellow Muslim, adultery and fornication and backbiting of a good Muslim. We have already discussed the punishments for these transgressions.

3. The unpardonable sin is *'shirk'* which means to put any thing or anybody on the same level as or in place of Allah. The penalty is execution.

To understand the difference in sin-perception, one has to understand that Christianity is a 'guilt-religion'. Guilt plays an important role in the whole question of salvation. A clear conscience is the goal, and it is reached by confession of sin and belief in the forgiveness of God.

In Islam shame and honour are significant issues. Acts that bring dishonour on a person or the family, losing face in front of others, are not only unwanted; they can have gruesome consequences.

A Muslim who makes mistakes perceives no need for a saviour. He seeks instructions from the Kor'an and the sheikhs. As the last prophet of Allah, Muhammad was sent to guide, illuminate and warn people.

The Christian believes that sin is rebellion against God. For him there is hope only in salvation through Jesus Christ, who gave his life for mankind to atone for sin. This forgiveness is a gift granted in mercy. Another essential element in the Christian faith is that by the help of the Holy Spirit the Christian is born again and enjoys a renewal of mind. A schematic comparison of the understanding of sin in the Bible and the Kor'an would look something like this:

Do humans have a sinful nature?

Christian: Everyone is born in sin, which explains a person's sinful nature and his tendency to sin (Rom. 5:12, 19).

Muslim: Everyone is born sinless and without a natural, sinful nature.

Is sin law breaking?
Christian: Sin in human nature causes a man to do evil (James 1:14, 15; Gen. 8:21; Rom. 6:12-14). It is rebellion against God (Psa. 51:3, 4). It is more than simply breaking God's law (1 John 3:24).
Muslim: Sin is breaking Allah's law (7v33). The harm is only against one's self (7v22), for Allah is too majestic to be affected.

How many have sinned?
Christian: All (except Jesus) have sinned and thus become guilty before God (Rom. 3:23).
Muslim: If Allah had wanted, he could have kept man from sinning (33v13; 13v31; 6v39).

Do sins affect the deity?
Christian: Sin grieves God (Gen. 6:5, 6; Psa. 78:40).
Muslim: Sin does not grieve Allah, who is too great to be affected. Allah created man's evil deeds, and man must do them (37v96; 54v49; 9v51; 57v22).

Does sin break fellowship?
Christian: Sin breaks fellowship between man and God and between man and man (1 John 1:3, 6, 7; Isa. 59:2, 3).
Muslim: Sin breaks only a law, not a fellowship such as between a son and his father.

Does the deity hate sin and sinners?
Christian: God hates sin, but loves sinners and wants them to repent (Rom. 5:6-8).
Muslim: Allah does not love evildoers (7v55; 42v40; 2v276).

What is the role of good deeds?
Christian: Good deeds do not earn forgiveness from God. Forgiveness is a free gift from God, and good deeds are

done in gratitude (Eph. 2:8, 9; Gal. 2:16).
Muslim: Good deeds, balanced against evil deeds in the Judgement Day, may help a person to get forgiveness (21v47, 25v70).

How are sins forgiven?
Christian: God forgives the sins of all who trust in Christ (2 Cor. 5:19-21. Christians can know this now (1 John 1:9; 2:12).
Muslim: Allah forgives whom he will and punishes whom he will (3v124; 5v118).

The Muslim believes he is a sinner solely because of his wrong deeds. He does not have a belief in original sin or the human inclination to wrongdoing. When he sins he does not feel that a relationship with Allah has been broken. That relationship is not as a son to a father. It is more to be compared with a slave's relationship to his master. It is a question of law more than love. He does not feel that he has offended Allah.

The conception of salvation

The Christian believes that salvation is a free gift. It is bestowed on sinful men and women by the grace and love of God. It is never deserved but accepted by simple faith. The love of God leads the sinner to repentance, conversion and a new birth. In this state the sinner is accepted by God and grows in sanctification.

Islam preaches that salvation is to be saved from 'hell' and given access to 'paradise'. In other words it is really a question of geography. More like a rescue. Salvation in Islam is obtained by:
1. Repentance that means one returns to a state of obedience.
2. Belief in Allah and obedience to the teaching of Muhammad.
3. Good deeds in accordance with the Five Pillars and Islamic Law.

In Islam good deeds are as important for salvation as faith. But good deeds are no assurance of salvation. Only Allah grants salvation. Man does not know his will.

A comparison of some Muslim and Christian concepts of salvation:

How is salvation assured?
Christian: Man has salvation because God desires to give it, because Christ died to make it possible, and because He has promised to give salvation to all who trust him for it.
Muslim: Allah's will for man cannot be known, and man may have salvation only if Allah wills for him to have it.

How is salvation obtained?
Christian: Salvation is brought about by a divine act; God, acting in Christ, has made it possible.
Muslim: Human actions help to get salvation.

Is salvation by faith or works?
Christian: Salvation is accepted by faith in Christ, and obtained apart from any human merit.
Muslim: Good works are as important as belief towards salvation.

What is a person saved from?
Christian: Salvation is from sin, its penalty and its power.
Muslim: Salvation is escape (or release) from the torture of hell, which is the penalty for sinful deeds.

What changes are the results of salvation?
Christian: Salvation is the change of heart, both spiritually and morally.
Muslim: Salvation is the change of place, a physical improvement (paradise instead of hell).

Can a person be sure of salvation?
Christian: Salvation is a present reality as well as a future hope. Christians may know that their sins are forgiven.

Heaven begins now and is completed after death at the Second Coming of Christ when God brings about his kingdom.

Muslim: Salvation is a future hope, for in this world a Muslim cannot know for certain whether Allah has destined him to paradise or hell.

Conclusion

Muslims have arrived in the West to stay. Their numbers will grow year by year. Politicians can to some extent decide how many will cross their borders. They are also able, to a degree, to ensure that their welfare systems are not exploited and that the few whose intent is to abuse their hospitality as a base for terror and violence are isolated and hindered in their activities. The Muslims, however, are here and will steadily grow in numbers, even if immigration is stopped. The Islamic rule against birth control will make sure that they will grow.

Europeans have personal views and political convictions as to how elected authorities should handle this challenge. They are able to express their points of view through the ballot box.

In addition to political responsibilities, citizens of host countries also have a Christian duty formulated by their Christian confession. A duty which means that their attitude towards Muslim immigrants must go beyond what is merely political and judicial.

There are two special areas where Christians in this new situation should have a separate agenda. We have already discussed the first – how we treat Muslims who are our neighbours, workmates and fellow citizens. This is a very practical matter.

Unfortunately, we discover that many people have double standards in these matters. Officially, a 'politically correct' position is expressed, that we all have to work for the full integration of all non-Europeans inside our borders. We should grant them the help and assistance they need. We should treat them with friendliness and understanding. They should have the benefits of our welfare systems. However, sometimes the Christian's attitude towards immigrants is less positive if they are Muslim. Muslims have been kept down in work places and are often treated as second-class citizens, if not officially, then personally.

Such attitudes are unworthy of Christians, whose laws are based on the biblical principle of love for neighbours and spontaneous help for the deserving and worthy poor. The first question should not be where the neighbour came from or how and why he came to their shores. It should be a question of personal responsibility towards him.

We have an outstanding example in the New Testament in the story of the Good Samaritan. He was engaged in positive and active help to the man who had fallen into the hands of highway robbers and left at the roadside. The Samaritan not only gave him much needed first aid. He also paid the innkeeper in advance so that further assistance was secured if required. This parable sets the standard for Christians in their relationships with strangers (Luke 10:25-37).

The other question Christians have to deal with is the biblical (theological) challenge that Islam poses to Christianity. How do we perceive Islam? What is the role of Islam as a world religion? The Christian points of views have been shaped and passed on in many different forms and changed numerous times since the seventh century. The viewpoints were to some extent developed by people who had contact with Muslims and were based on practical experiences in the field. These on occasions often took place in co-operation with Muslims. As a result these missionaries generally had a more positive and open attitude towards Islam.

A Christian theology on the question of Islam was, however, also perfected in academic strongholds, usually some distance from where the two religions met face to face. It was often in those strongholds that controversial viewpoints came to the fore. However, even there apologetic perspective was developed.

Generally speaking, Christian responses to Islam manifest themselves in three main attitudes:

1. Some liberal Christians view Islam favourably, if only because it is a monotheistic religion. In addition, in the Kor'an there are many biblical motifs. Jews, Christians and Muslims all have Abraham as their father spiritually and, perhaps, physically too. The Muslim accepts Jesus Christ as a great prophet. Christians and Muslims also have similar ethical principles. Liberal Christians might not attempt to convert the Muslims. Rather they would work with Muslims for a better society.

2. Evangelical Christians, while favouring Islam as a monotheistic religion, would stress that there is no salvation in Islam. Among other things, Islam denies the core of the Gospel, Jesus Christ, the Son of God, his crucifixion and resurrection. Muslims, however, are our brothers and sisters. Muhammad disposed of the many idols in the *Ka'aba* and introduced the belief in one god, Allah. Evangelical Christians would take the view that their task is to proclaim and explain Jesus Christ to them.

3. On the extreme right of Christianity are those who claim that Islam is an anti-Christian religion. Muhammad was a false prophet and the Kor'an a forgery, they have argued.

In support of this point of view they quote, among others, the words of John in his epistles, where he writes that the sign of anti-Christ is that it denies that Jesus is Christ (Saviour) and that there is a Father and a Son (1 John 2:18-23; 4:1-3; 2 John 4:7). Conservative Christians would take the view that they must be on their guard against that religion and combat it with the sword of the Word. They have also persuaded many other Christians to adopt the conservative viewpoint.

A religious system can be analysed, and approved or evaluated as false and dangerous. On the other hand, adherents of any religion should be respected as fellow human beings and appreciated as individuals. All persons, irrespective of their colour, religious affiliation or political convictions, have value as they are of concern to the Gospel message and embraced by the Great Commission. It should always be maintained that racism is unchristian and unbiblical. However, to stand up for the right teaching and principles is both Christian and biblical.

To a Muslim a persuasive and valuable testimony to Christian belief is that Christians are close to them, sensitive to their religion and experience. It is important that we reveal a willingness to serve and appreciate what God, in his love, has done for all people. We must always have in mind that our task is to witness and not condemn. We should, as part of our belief system, accept that it is possible to be a missionary without attacking.

Western society is pluralistic and characterised by a variety of political movements. Nationals and Muslims are involved in both the positive and the negative aspects of the culture clashes that result. In all this there is a need for a decisive Christian influence in an attempt to find the balance between political and national interest and Christian ideals. This balance is, perhaps, only arrived at by an examination of Christian principles. It is not a balance between being a British, African or American citizen and being a Christian. It is a balance that requires us to be a British, African or American Christian.

Bibliography

Aagaard, Johannes. 'Da verden skiftede gear.' *Den Nye Dialogue.* 86 (December 2001): 3–5.

Arendt, Niels Henrik. *Gud er stor! Om islam of kristendom.* Frederiksberg, Denmark: Anis, 1994.

Andersen, Poul Erik. 'Et kulturmøde.' *Præsteforeningens Blad.* 89 (November 1999/47): 1070–1078.

Anderson, Norman. *Islam in the Modern World.* Leicester, UK: Apollos, 1990.

El-Awa, Mohammed S. *Punishment in Islamic Law.* Indianapolis: USA: American Trust Publications, 1982.

Glasse, Cyril. *Concise Dictionary of Islam.* San Francisco, USA: Harper and Row, 1989.

Jomier, Jaques. *How To Understand Islam.* London, UK: SCM Press, 1988.

Kateregga, B D and David Shenk. *Islam and Christianity.* Nairobi, Kenya: Uzima Press, 1980.

Marshall, Paul, Roberta Green and Lela Gilbert. I*slam at the Crossroads.* Grand Rapids, MI.: Baker Books, 2002.

McCurry, Don. *Healing the Broken Family of Abraham.* Colorado Springs, USA: Ministries to Muslims, 2002.

Pittelkow, Ralf. *Efter 11. September.*

Siddiqi, Mohammed Iqbal. *The Penal Law of Islam.* Delhi, India: International Islamic Publishers, 1994.

Van Donzel. E. *Islamic Desk Reference.* Leiden, the Netherlands: E, J. Brill, 1994.

VanGerpen, Emory. *Notes On Islam.* Singapore: Oasis Books, 1974.

J.Dudley Woodberry, ed. *Muslims and Christians on the Emmaus Road.* Monrovia, USA: MARC, 1989.

Kor'an Translation.

An- Nabawiyah and Mushaf Al-Madinah. *The Holy Qur-án. English Translation of the Meanings and Commentary.* Medina, Saudi Arabia: King Fahd Holy Qur-án Printing Complex, n.d.